Street Crossers

Street Crossers

*Conversations with Simple Church Planters
and Stories of Those Who Send Them*

RICK SHROUT

WIPF & STOCK · Eugene, Oregon

STREET CROSSERS
Conversations with Simple Church Planters and Stories of Those Who Send Them

Wipf & Stock
An Imprint of Wipf and Stock Publishers
199 W. 8th Ave., Suite 3
Eugene, OR 97401
www.wipfandstock.com

ISBN 13: 978-1-4982-6043-5
Manufactured in the U.S.A.

In Memory of William C. Shrout Jr.:
Father, friend, mentor, and unwavering example
of how to walk the Jesus way.

And to Toni:
Companion, encourager, "butterfly," and shining beacon of hope and grace
in the midst of life's trials and difficulties.

Contents

Foreword

SOME OF JESUS' LAST words to us were these: "Go into all the world and preach the gospel to every creature" (Matt. 26:18). If our field is the world, does this not make us all *world* missionaries?

Not so fast on that "world" front. Yes, the "Great Commission" is a global one. And we are called to be "global missionaries," even "global citizens of planet Earth," as some are calling it. But we can be so "global" that we can't see across the street. Or as the rap on academics has it, we can love everybody in general so much that we love nobody in particular very much. One of my favorite humorists was George Carlin. But I was never sure whether Carlin loved the humans he made such fun of. In fact, one of the easiest ways of loving people is to avoid their company.

Or at least avoid crossing the street. Rick Shrout calls us to start reading Jesus' last words as a call to be what he delightfully and mischievously calls "street crossers." We all need to begin our "world mission" somewhere. So why not start simply and locally? The glory of the local church is that it's global. But the only way to the global is through the local. You can't universalize until you first particularize. You can't cross life's Rubicons until you first cross the street.

Of course, you don't go to the other extreme and love only the particular at the expense of the universal. Clergyman Jonathan Swift wrote in November 1725 to Alexander Pope a famous letter. On the eve of the publication of his classic satire on human nature called *Gulliver's Travels* (1726), he asked his friend to do him a favor:

> When you think of the world give it one lash the more at my request. I have ever hated all nations, professions, and communities, and all my love is towards individuals: for instance, I hate the tribe of lawyers, but I love Counsellor Such-a-one and Judge Such-a-one . . . But principally I hate and detest that animal called man, although I heartily love John, Peter, Thomas, and

so forth. This is the system upon which I have governed myself many years, but do not tell.[1]

Hungarian novelist and anti-totalitarian crusader Arthur Koestler built his anti-totalitarian crusades on his opposition to dissolving the single person into the hive mentality of the community and to refuse to believe that the individual "is the result of a crowd of a million divided by a million." At one point Koestler even confessed, "I don't believe any more in humanity. I believe in the individual."[2]

In this exciting and useful book *Street Crossers*, Shrout shows how the universal can be found in the vernacular. We are all writing the stories of our lives from common plot-lines of feelings, experiences, and thoughts while each person adds a unique twist that makes their story uniquely individual. But I can't say it any better than Shrout has in his introduction:

> To be a follower of Jesus, to be his disciple, is to be on a mission. It is to be a missionary to the other side. Street crossers are people who "cross" the street for the sake of Christ and the world. In their going—in their "crossing" of the street—they make the sign of the cross by becoming a bridge from one world to another. That crossing is both sacrificial and sacramental.

What I loved most about this amazing book is that *Street Crossers* will show you how to make sure that when you "cross over" to the other side you still take the cross over.

Leonard Sweet
Drew University,
George Fox University,
sermons.com

1. Quoted by P. N. Furbank, "Misreading Gulliver," *Times Literary Supplement*: 12 November 2010, 16.

2. As quoted by Michael Scammell, "Koestler the Dangerous Intellectual," *Times Literary Supplement*: 21 July 2010, 5.

Acknowledgments

L IKE ALL "ORIGINAL" THOUGHTS, they do not exist without the minds that precede them. This is no less true of the ideas behind this book. Its content would not exist without the stories of the people behind the ministries described within these pages. I chose four stories to include in *Street Crossers* from among dozens of interviews, so there are many more experiences and journeyers to which I am indebted. All are worthy of recognition and would serve to challenge and inspire, if those stories were told. My appreciation goes to the following workers in the kingdom: Chuck Allen, Tom Anthony, Bill Bean, Harold Behr, Mike Bishop, Peter Bunton, Mark Burton, Joseph Cartwright, Guy Caskey, Neil Cole, Galen Currah, Tony Dale, Marcus Dorsey, Trey Doty, Robert Fitts, Jason Evans, Donald Gingras, Rich Hagler, Jim Herrington, Alan Hirsch, D. G. Hollums, Darin Horst, Jess Hutchison, Dan Jansen, Glenn Johnson, Jason Johnston, Aaron Klinefelter, Nate Krupp, Dan Mayhew, Wayne Martin, Chris Marshall, Rachelle Mee-Chapman, Kenny Moore, David Nicholson, Susan Olson, Amy Palmer, George Patterson, Tom Planck, Kevin Rains, Rob Robinson, Alex Ryan, Steve Schroepfer, Rick Scruggs, Keith Shields, Ken Shuman, Brian Simmons, Glenn Smith, Danae Stewart, Michael Stoltzfus, Rose Swetman, Doug & Becky Taylor, Bill Tenny-Brittian, John White, Jeff Wright, and Greg Yoder. I probably forgot someone, so a special thanks goes out to you, too.

A big word of thanks goes out to Brad Taylor, my editor for *Street Crossers*. His eye for detail was amazing . . . finding numerous grammatical errors, typos, and fuzzy wording, even after I thought the manuscript had been sifted clean. We crossed paths via our mutual connection to George Fox University. *Street Crossers* is the culmination of my doctoral studies at GFU, so I want to thank Kent Yinger for his guidance as my dissertation advisor; Leonard Sweet for his love of words and for setting the bar at writing scores of books in the time it took me to write one; Loren Kerns for his watchful eye; and to the brothers of my doctoral cohort—thanks to Tony Blair for his encouragement that kept me going, to Winn Griffin for his "fatherly prodding" when I needed a swift kick— and to the rest of the pack who raised me up from a valley of ecclesial cynicism to a hilltop where I could see hope for the church once again: Rick Bartlett, Jason Clark, Rick Hans, George Hemingway, Todd Hunter, Randy Jumper, Eric Keck, Nick Howard, Mike McNichols, Ken Niles, Craig Oldenburg, Rob Seewald, Dwight Spotts, and David Wollenburg.

Lastly, thanks to my greatest sources of inspiration—Toni Shrout, my wife, and my father, Bill Shrout. Both battled cancer during the writing of this book. Toni continues her fight to this day (July 15, 2011). My father passed from life to life on August 25, 2009. Their fight and determination served as an incredible example and motivation to finally finish my doctoral journey and ultimately this book. Without them, you wouldn't have this book to read.

Introduction

IT USED TO BE that Christian missionaries would set sail for foreign lands on long ocean voyages. Today it takes a passport, vaccinations, and hopping aboard an international flight to end up on the mission field. But the times they are a-changin'. If you live in the United States or Canada and want to travel to a foreign mission field to share the gospel of Jesus, there is no need to get onboard a ship or purchase airfare online at Expedia.com. All you need to do is cross the street.

There are mission fields across the street from your house. There are mission fields across the street from your house of worship. These mission fields are as close and green as the lawn next door. Many of these mission fields could be considered "foreign." The culture within these nearby homes may be very different from yours in many respects. Though you live in the same neighborhood or within the same city limits, your view of the world and the way you live your life can be worlds apart from those who live next door or work across the street. It is very possible that your view of the world and theirs—your worldviews—are polar opposites. You may see things from a "northern perspective," while your neighbor sees things from a "southern perspective." And I'm not just whistling Dixie here. We are talking about opinions, values, and lifestyles that clash and have difficulty coexisting. We are talking about a growing cultural divide between the haves and the have-nots—those who have a lifestyle based on the cultural mores of a church-world and those who do not. There is a strange and different world from yours out there . . . across the street.

It is very common in the church to think that to be involved in the work of missions requires sending a trained missionary to a foreign field, to a country and culture very different from our own. To be a missionary in these foreign lands requires cross-cultural awareness, sensitivity, perspective, understanding, and a non-judgmental attitude. It is no different when we speak about reaching out to those who live in a different culture even when they live or work next door or across the street. It takes a cross-cultural missionary to go there. It takes a street crosser.

STREET CROSSERS: A NEW KIND OF MISSIONARY

What are street crossers? Who are they? Why do we need them and what is their purpose? First of all, street crossers are ministers of the gospel. They are not jaywalkers, because they cross streets at appropriate times and places. They look for the signals and pay close attention to them. They are aware of the law of the land and the lay of the land on the other side of the street. They understand that the land they seek to enter across the street is different from the land and culture from which they come.

Street crossers are those who literally and metaphorically cross the street to reach the other side—but not simply to answer the proverbial riddle of why the chicken does the same thing. Street crossers cross the street *to reach people* who live on the other side. They cross over the street in order to enter another world, a world very different from the one most of us church-acculturated people live in. They are world-go-to-ers. In these different worlds, street crossers seek to enter into the lives and the affairs of "normal people," at least normal on the other side of the street.[1] In our church-world on our side of the street, we might think of or refer to them as "abnormal," "non-Christians," "un-churched," "unbelievers," or even "sinners." On their side of the street, those references are often offensive and irrelevant. In their eyes *we* are the abnormal ones. So street crossers see those on the other side as normal, endowed with the divine image, and dearly loved by God.

Philosophers, historians, and cultural observers often use the term "postmodern" to describe many of the normal people who live across the street. Your neighbor next door could possibly be one of "them." But whether or not he or she fits the profile of a postmodern is somewhat beside the point.[2] Postmodern or otherwise, pockets of diverse cultures are scattered across our communities.

---

1. Sweet, *Jesus Drives Me Crazy*, 13.

2. Defining "postmodern" or "postmodernity" is no easy task. For the purposes of this book, think of it as a point of view and ensuing way of life that questions traditional institutions and their related value systems. Think of it as a foreign culture . . . having the characteristic of a different country or language other than your own . . . strange and unfamiliar.

If street crossers are people who both literally and metaphorically cross streets, then the same can be said for streets—they are both literal and metaphorical for this discussion. A street is a literal pathway, a road composed of dirt, gravel, concrete, or asphalt. Streets lead to a connection.

But streets also create disconnections. They serve as dividing lines between homes, between businesses, between different demographical areas in towns and cities. They section off institutions, businesses, school districts, and gangs. Streets divide and separate people from other people. Streets serve as boundaries . . . between homes, families, cultures, and worlds. And when a boundary is crossed, a collision occurs. Different worlds collide . . . dissimilar worlds intersect. Yet miraculously, in the midst of the collision, two worlds also come together. It takes a street crosser to bring divergent worlds together, and this happens when they follow Jesus into the streets and on to the other side.

"Crossers" are those who take up their crosses and follow after Christ. They cross the street because they see Jesus calling to them from the other side and so they follow. To be a follower of Jesus, to be his disciple, is to be on a mission. It is to be a missionary to the other side. Street crossers are people who "cross" the street for the sake of Christ and the world. In their going—in their "crossing" of the street—they make the sign of the cross by becoming a bridge from one world to another. That crossing is both sacrificial and sacramental.

In a sacrificial way, street crossers lay down their comfortable church-world preferences in order to enter the world and preferences of others, the culture of normal people who live across the street. In a sacramental way, street crossers make the sign of the cross by demonstrating the way of the kingdom on the other side of the street where people can actually see and hear a real-life Jesus follower. Street crossers are signposts in this sense—signifiers that point to the Signified, the king of another reality, another world, and another culture—the kingdom of God. A street crosser is one who will give up that others might live up, and one who will be a cross-bearer that others might see the One who bears their cross. Street crossers represent Jesus as a citizen of his kingdom while they live in the context of a culture other than their own. This describes a street crosser. This describes a missionary. This describes a Jesus follower.

We might say that street crossers take the kingdom with them on their journey, or perhaps more amazingly, they take Jesus with them and in them. At the same time, it is Jesus who takes them. Think about it. If we are his followers, we go where he goes. It is truly a humbling thought to realize that street crossers, and all followers of Jesus, are the representatives of Christ. Wherever we are, he is. Even more sobering: Wherever he is, we are invited to follow . . . even to the uttermost parts of the earth . . . across the street.

WHAT IS THIS BOOK ABOUT?

This book is about street crossers of a particular kind. They have two distinct characteristics unique to the theme of this book. First, they are simple church planters (a definition to follow shortly). Second, these simple church planters desire to stay connected with their faith tradition.[3] They request the encouragement and support of a traditional church or denomination to assist them in their church planting. As you read their stories, you will sense their vision, passion, and understanding of the purpose and mission of the church. You will discover that much of their "success" is a direct result of those who come alongside them to lend support and make it possible for them to go into all the world—the world across the street—as local missionaries.

The kind of street crossers you will read about in this book plant and establish simple churches and networks. For our discussion, a "simple church" is a small community of Jesus followers who are committed to one another and to being a positive presence in their neighborhood. They like to keep it simple. Albert Einstein supposedly said, "Everything should be made as simple as possible, but not simpler."[4] Simple church planters enthusiastically embrace the KISS principle: "Keep it simple, stupid." Jocularity aside, a more philosophical perspective is offered by German-born American abstract expressionist Hans Hofmann: "The ability to simplify means to eliminate the unnecessary so the necessary may speak."[5] Did Hofmann have the body of Christ in mind when he

---

3. There has been a tendency in the past of simple church planters, or "house church-ers," to leave the institutional church nest altogether in a protest against its perceived shortcomings. This is not the case for the simple church planters portrayed in this book or the kind of street crosser this book advocates.

4. Hiroshi, "What is Occam's Razor?"

5. Hofmann, "Hans Hofmann Quotes."

said this? Not likely, but his comment fits the heart and mind of simple church planters perfectly. Simple church planters believe that much of what we hold to as essential for church life is actually unnecessary, especially when it comes to cross-cultural ministry to people unaccustomed to or uninterested in Christianity and "church-as-usual." The "essentials" sometimes impede the necessary things from happening, such as mission and the call to go across the street, for example. The move toward simplicity is what gives this particular kind of church planter the mobility and freedom to invest more time, energy, and resources in ministry and relationships to those on both sides of the street. The stories you read about here illustrate this point.

But the move toward simplicity is, ironically, no simple task. It gets complicated. This is true of all relationships. Church life, be it traditional or simple, is also complex—on several levels, at the very least. First of all, if church life is exactly that—a life form—then like any other life form there is more than meets the eye. Any microbiologist will tell you that even the simplest of single-cell organisms is a complex yet harmonious network of biological systems and relationships. This is infinitely more so for a multi-celled organism, such as the human body, that is reportedly comprised of as many as 100 trillion cells. That's 100 million *million* cells all working together for the common good of the body! The apostle Paul teaches that followers of Jesus make up Christ's body with each "member" contributing and making it possible for the entire body to simply function.[6] Each person brings to the ecclesial table a set of emotional, social, historical, and cultural building materials by which the "complex" of Christ is constructed and connected together. And, given the increasing diversity of the global human village, it feels more complex all the time. But this is not cause for despair; rather, it is but one facet of the mystery of the gospel. We behold the beauty of the body of Christ in both its simplicity and its complexity . . . in its "simplexity."[7]

If the relational life of the Church is so complex, what, then, is "simple" about the simple church? It's how they organize or structure

6. 1 Corinthians 12:12–13.

7. Simplexity is an interdisciplinary term and emerging theory that proposes an interdependent relationship between simplicity and complexity. Anuraj Gambhir is often credited with popularizing the term in his conversations surrounding mobile technology. In 2008, Jeffery Kluger wrote about the growing interest in the paradoxical relationship between simplicity and complexity across diverse disciplines of study. See Kuger, *Simplexity*.

themselves for relationship. For instance, simple churches will have leadership, but it may not consist of formal roles and titles. And, instead of building and caring for church facilities, they gather and meet just about anywhere (typically in homes, which already have spaces dedicated for day-to-day living in relationship). Often simple church folk make reference to house churches when describing themselves.[8] But to emphasize the house is to miss the remarkable adaptability of simple churches. Meeting in a house does not necessarily make things simple, nor does it ensure that such a gathering is more in line with a New Testament "model" of doing church (an issue and concern of some house church proponents, but not the focus of this book). Simple church advocates believe that relationships, calling, and mission are central to the identity and functioning of the church. They believe the home and other more intimate and natural settings are conducive for establishing and nurturing these relationships. Relationship to God and to one another as a committed community of faith fuels the ability to be on a mission to the world. Perhaps the Blues Brothers said it right—"We're on a mission from God" . . . to the uttermost parts of the earth . . . to the world across the street.[9]

How big is your world? What is your sphere of influence? Maybe you have heard of the trivia game called "Six Degrees of Kevin Bacon," in which players connect actors and their movie appearances with Kevin Bacon's movies. It's based on the small world phenomenon and the phrase "six degrees of separation," which suggests everyone in the world is connected by no more than six connecting relationships. That is amazing! But let's pay attention to the first degree, and then maybe the second. If you lift your arms straight out from your side, what world do you touch? Jesus said to "go into all the world" (Mark 16:15). I believe he first meant the world you can touch from where you are standing, from where you are living. That's what Jesus did. Be a world-go-to-er. It's much like being a street crosser. Jesus could have easily said, "Go cross the street into all the world." Crossing the street leads to another world, a world with cultures different from your own, a world with people different from you regarding values and perspectives.

8. Though the term house church is common, simple churches are also referred to by other names. Some additional terms referred to are organic churches, organic fellowships, small missional communities of faith, and micro-churches.

9. See Acts 1:8.

Street crossers, simple church planters, world-go-to-ers, and missionaries have at least one thing in common—they respond to Christ's call to go. It does not have to be a "far-going" to be a legitimate response. A "far distance" can be as close as the house next door. Instead of measuring distance in miles or kilometers, we need to think in terms of measuring the distance between worldviews, languages, values, and lifestyles. This distance, this gap, can be huge, even when looking at the neighbor across the street.

Most people, normal or otherwise, believe it's not worth the effort to close the gap. If so, don't wait for these people to come to your Sunday morning service. Some will never walk through a church door even though they live directly across the street or across town. They will not walk across the street to enter into your world, especially your church-world. A church-world is a foreign culture to them and they have no interest whatsoever in learning how to speak the language and respect church customs. For example, our language can be quite strange and difficult to understand for normal people, even most Christians, for that matter. It's been referred to by some as "Christianese." One example of Christianese is seen in our fondness for "-tion" words . . . salvation, justification, reconciliation, redemption, sanctification, glorification, etc. Our customs and beliefs come across as antiquated and narrow-minded. For example, on our side of the street, we talk about heaven, divine glory, and life after death. Normal people talk about earth, global warming, and life after taxes. Yet another example is when it comes to the custom of marriage. We say, "It's between one man and one woman, and abstain from sexual promiscuity before marriage." Normal people ask, "If two people are committed to one another and love one another, what's wrong with that? And besides, kicking a tire or two and going for a test drive before you commit makes sense." Not only is our Christian language difficult to understand, so is our perspective on personal behavior and lifestyle. It's a cultural perspective most normal people would rather not learn and embrace. But that's what missionaries do—they learn to speak the language and appreciate a different culture. That's what street crossers do—they choose to go and live in a strange new world.

MISSIONS-MINDED OR MISSIONAL?

"Missional" has become a popular buzzword these days in discussions about the calling of the church. Just Google it and see for yourself. I wholeheartedly embrace its specific nuance and intended meaning. But what concerns me is dreaded overkill. Fresh words tend to lose their original dynamic as they become familiar and marketed as the latest and greatest spiritual insights to come down the pike. Repackaged words and expressions often become faddish when assimilated into pop-church cultural jargon. The words become powerless hand-me-downs. If this is inevitable, it should give us cause to be on the lookout for new ways to describe eternal and divine principles. The transformational power of a principle is often unleashed when we discover it as if for the first time.

Most of us are very familiar with the words "mission" and "missions"—common hand-me-down words in the church. Sadly, we are so acquainted with these two words that many of us use the terms casually, disconnecting ourselves from the implications of mission as a calling on each one of our lives and as congregations. I believe this is becoming true of the word "missional." This term came along at a time in recent church history that brought about a new sense of what we are to be about as followers of Jesus. Each of us is called to be on mission in the world as his representative and minister. But I'm afraid the term is already losing its original divine gusto; it is bandied about as if the average person knows what it means. So before you forget, let me again remind you what being missional means—it means crossing the street.

One of the best definitions for the word missional that I have ever heard comes from house church connoisseur Wolfgang Simson. I was attending a house church conference in Vancouver, British Columbia. Simson was addressing questions about the role of house churches within the discussion of what it means to be missional. He defined a healthy house church as a small group of Christians capable of vital ministry that address both the needs of the group and those of their community. After he said this, he paused momentarily as if to reflect on what he just described . . . then rephrased his definition and said, "Holistic missional entities: It basically boils down to loving your neighbor."[10]

"Love your neighbor." This is simple, perhaps—but also one of the most difficult and costly things we can ever choose to do. For a moment, just set all the theological debates aside, place all the books on missiology and the missional church back on the shelf, and turn off all the mp3 and podcast discussions on the topic. Our theorizing and pontifications about what it means to be a missional church really does boil down to

10. Wolfgang Simson, Vancouver House Church Conference, November 17–18, 2003.

loving our neighbor. Can you think of a more telling and convincing way to communicate the gospel no matter the cultural context? So here it is again: The first step in loving our neighbor is the step off our own curb and into the street.

Some have suggested that there is a difference between being "missions-minded" and being "missional."[11] Being missions-minded is to *support* missionary work. Being missional is to *do* missionary work. They may have a point. After all, it's much easier to be missions-minded and support someone else to do the work of a missionary than it is to do the work ourselves. Recording artist Scott Wesley Brown wrote a telling song about how we tend to avoid the mission field to which God calls us because we fear the challenges and costs in going . . . or in crossing. In the song, Brown uses the stereotypical reference of Africa that has come to embody the challenges of overseas missions. Quite often, Africa is flippantly used to represent a radically different culture from our own here in the church of North America. Africa is seen to be a strange world that poses immense dangers. But the reality is, you don't have to travel halfway around the globe to find a strange, uncomfortable, or even threatening world. To be certain, in the major urban centers of North America, and even in suburbia, you will find great challenges and an increasing number of "natives" who speak a different language than your own. Just walk across the street and see for yourself.

I do not believe we need to make a choice between being missions-minded and being missional, nor do I suggest that one is more desirable than the other. Both are good. Both are needed. Both are valuable. And simple church planters need missions-minded people and congregations to stand behind them and to send more street crossers. That's the purpose of this book: to share the stories of street crossers and those who choose to stand by them, support them, and walk with them—even across the street.

If you choose not to go, or you feel you are unprepared to go because you don't understand the culture or speak the language, then find a potential street crosser and do everything in your power to lend a hand. They are willing, ready, and eager to go—with your help. Chances are your church is already involved in a similar kind of support ministry. It's called supporting cross-cultural missionaries. And chances are your local church body truly loves giving and lending support in this way. This

11. See Stetzer, *Planting Missional Churches*; and Minatrea, *Shaped by God's Heart*.

commitment to support is demonstrated in a very unique way. In all my years of being part of the body of Christ, in just about every church building I've ever been in, one commonality and feature stands out in my mind—bulletin boards!

All over the country, these cork-covered communication contraptions are proudly displayed with a patchwork of photos and maps of missionaries and the countries in which they serve. This gives me hope. That hope is not simply knowing that the church at large is willing to give in order for others to serve where they cannot. That hope is also envisioning the incredible potential of the countless churches across the land coming alongside street crossers—simple church planters. The possibilities are virtually endless, even for churches struggling to find ways to keep their doors open. You can partner with them in a local ministry in very powerful and transformational ways. Your church already has the resources and tested capacity needed to reach out to an emerging and changing culture—a culture that is transforming your neighborhood, for better or worse. You can participate in the mission. You can help make a difference and play a vital role in demonstrating the culture of the kingdom before the eyes of a church-rejecting culture by sending and supporting simple church planters across the street as local missionaries right in your own town.

WHAT YOU WILL FIND IN THIS BOOK

What you will find in these true-life accounts are people who desire to follow Christ in ministry to the world around them. They have chosen to do so by planting simple churches. As noted, some of these simple churches meet in homes, but they also gather in just about any place you can imagine . . . offices, coffee shops, backyards, schools, and even in church buildings. Location may vary, but their overall goals and purposes are similar—to remain simple and streamlined, to invest more in relationship building than in church buildings.

These simple church planters sometimes establish networks of simple churches. Networks are typically a connection between church plants for the purpose of support and training. They grow as a result of simple churches reaching new people and deciding to start another simple church. Sometimes a new church starts from within the circle of friends of new people. Sometimes they start from within a simple church by sending a person or small group of people from the existing group to go and plant a new faith community. Networks also develop as a result of the original simple church planter sensing a call to plant more churches.

In this book, you will enjoy the stories of four specific simple church planting ministries and the street crossers who lead them. You will discover the churches and denominations that lend support in a variety of ways. Their support comes in the form of prayer, manpower, finances, training, commissioning, and the empowerment that comes in simply acknowledging that what street crossers are doing is valuable and important. Their journeys were obtained through interviews and compiled into stories. In this book, you will meet Chris Marshall of Ordinary Community Church in Cincinnati, Ohio (affiliated with Mideast Baptist Conference); Jason Evans of the Ecclesia Collective in San Diego, California (affiliated with the Pacific Southwest Mennonite Conference); Jess Hutchison and Marcus Dorsey of Winding Road Church of God in Portland, Oregon (affiliated with the Association of the Churches of God in Oregon and Southwest Washington); and Keith Shields of LifeHouse Christian Church in Vancouver, British Columbia (affiliated with Connections Christian Church network and Bow Valley Community Church in Calgary, Alberta).

Each narrative is followed by a portion of an actual interview with these remarkable individuals as well as some of my own reflections and encouragements for you to think more deeply. This section can also be used as a group study guide for initiating discussion around the idea of what it might look like and what it might require to support and send simple church planters across the street.

WHO SHOULD READ THIS BOOK AND WHY?

This book is intended to encourage simple church planters to be faithful to their calling and to pursue it within the context and support of their denominational tribes. Its purpose is to inform traditional church pastors and denominational leaders about the opportunity to partner with simple church planters. My aim is to inspire those who wonder about the ability of traditional churches to work hand-in-hand with alternative expressions of church life. This book is for congregations that feel challenged by and inadequately equipped to minister to their surrounding and changing cultural environments. Finally, it is for those who are critical of either church expression, be it traditional or simple. No one form or expression of church life is perfect. We are all in this thing we call the kingdom, so it behooves us to join hands and walk together.

When you finish reading, you might decide to write a new chapter by putting your arm around a street crosser and commission this brother or sister in the name of Jesus with your love, encouragement, prayer, and with every means of support you can give. As a simple church planter, you might decide to lay down your cynicism of the traditional church and reach out in humility to a pastor, a local church, or a denominational leader and admit you don't have all the answers, that you need their involvement, and that you want to partner with them for the sake of Christ and the world. But regardless of what role you play, get ready and prepare yourself as you read the stories of simple church planters. Listen to their heart cries. See if your heart cries out with the same desires . . . the same longings . . . the same sense of calling to be faithful to Christ, his body, and those on the other side of the street. Let their passion for Jesus and his kingdom and their commitment to those on the other side move you to action in your community. Take a walk across the street. Support your local missionary.

1

Simply Put

CHURCH-AS-USUAL WASN'T ENOUGH

CHRIS MARSHALL SAYS HE was "born into a church split" and describes himself as a "denominational mutt." On his father's side, his grandfather was the pastor of a large fundamentalist Baptist church in Philadelphia and surprisingly got involved in the charismatic movement in the 1970s. After his parents divorced, Chris was a "fundamentalist Baptist" three weeks a month while living with his mom, and a "charismatic" once a week when visiting his dad in a basement sanctuary where his grandfather was the pastor. Later in life, Chris found himself involved in ministry with other denominational expressions of the church. A denominational mutt is a very fitting self-description.

Chris remembers the church experiences with his grandfather as being positive. But after his grandfather died when Chris was in the fourth grade, his subsequent perceptions of Christianity were influenced by his mother through being exposed to a legalistic form of church life. As he grew older, Chris became disappointed by the hypocrisy he perceived in many professing Christians. But then came a turning point in his life. During his junior year in high school, a youth leader in Chris's church began spending time with him and a mentoring relationship ensued. "It was a life-on-life relationship. He was the first guy I ever knew who actually did what he said he believed in," Chris notes.

At the age of seventeen, Chris had another powerful experience. While driving his car on a rainy night, a feeling of love overwhelmed him—it was the presence of Jesus. A sudden flash of memories of Bible stories from his childhood flooded his mind. It was the moment when he first sensed a call to ministry. God was calling him to be an influence in the lives of others—the kind of influence he had longed for in his own life. He was convinced it was a calling to proclaim the gospel in a way that would have caught his attention had someone explained it to him in a relevant way.

Chris looks back and realizes that his confrontational approach to sharing his faith in high school was a byproduct of the kind of Christianity on which he had been weaned as a child. It was also a reflection of his "all-or-nothing" personality. Chris remembers:

> I was pretty bold. I wore a lot of Christian t-shirts like, "Hell Ain't Cool." Our church youth group had a program [called] Evangelism Explosion and I would use that on strangers, forcing my agenda on them. I was just pretty vocal and brash about my Christianity, not afraid to stand alone in my beliefs. It was later in life that I realized a lot of that was more about me than about the people I claimed I wanted to reach.

As an example of his zeal, Chris wanted to be a missionary to a foreign country where he could actually be persecuted for his faith. Commitment to Christ meant having a willingness to suffer and pay any price. He contemplated quitting high school and forgoing college so he could move overseas as quickly as possible. But this kind of thinking began to subside after he met his wife-to-be, Nicki, who attended the same youth group. They soon found themselves thinking about attending the same college after high school—Trinity College in Deerfield, Illinois (known now as Trinity International University). Both of them were high school athletes and turned down athletic scholarships to bigger colleges because they both sensed a call to ministry. They married after their sophomore year at Trinity.

While attending Trinity College, Chris served as a youth pastor in two different churches in Chicago. The first position he took was with a Disciples of Christ church, a denomination he knew nothing about. He simply showed up because they had an opening. The second position was with a non-denominational church. Like many young hopeful ministers, he had both positive and negative experiences in ministry. Chris likes to say that he had a perfect idea for the church, but there was not one church in existence that could match up to his ideals at that point in his life.

After college, Chris and Nicki moved to Kalamazoo, Michigan, where he was a youth pastor for three years at a Reformed church in nearby Portage. It was an experience he thoroughly enjoyed. While living in the Chicago area, he had been exposed to the Willow Creek model of ministry, and tried to incorporate this into youth ministry in Michigan. What happened over the next three years was almost beyond imagination. A network of youth ministries emerged from youth pastors working together. From this fellowship an area gathering developed— Community Youth Worship. It was a worship service for students and led by students. In just one year the service averaged between 1,500 and 2,000 students in a single evening, filling the largest theaters in the area. In the process, Chris had become the coordinator for this network of youth ministries. Chris recalls:

> It was kind of a heyday. We were experiencing this great stuff. But at the same time, inwardly, I was starting to die a little bit. All I can say is that when I was experiencing this success on the out- side, inwardly I was dying, absolutely dying. I was just trying to perform, perform, perform! But something was really not click- ing on the inside. . . . I think I completely lost track of my own relationship with God in the midst of the busyness and running the programs. The need to be creative and keep a busy sched- ule of activities left me spiritually, emotionally, and physically exhausted. But the spiritual exhaustion kept increasing which began to make me question everything I was doing. The ministry job seemed to be more about doing Christian industry rather than genuine ministry. I was running programs instead of do- ing life-on-life, which is how I am wired. Later, I realized as well that I had a kind of addiction to success. I needed it for my own personal worth and that's what I was doing in ministry. But the successes were becoming less and less fulfilling. They wouldn't satisfy. That's when I realized I needed a change; I needed to re-visit these issues with God. You get accolades in ministry for being busy and exciting, but when it came down to it, I needed to slow down and re-connect with God to become whole again.

Some of his associates advised Chris that he should pursue a great- er role in the church. But this was something he felt that he needed to consider with caution. Eventually, Chris and Nicki decided that the best thing to do was to get out of the way and leave. "I had burnt out in a couple of ways. I think I wanted to leave the ministry altogether. None of the churches had ever satisfied what I was looking for. I was chasing after something," Chris notes. In time, he came to understand what he was chasing:

> I realized I had gotten so depressed that I wanted to leave ministry, but I had developed a very high profile. So, I decided to go to seminary in order to leave the ministry, because I thought if I go to seminary, no one would ask me any questions. They'll just assume I'm taking the next step or something. But actually it just bought me some time.

In 1998, Chris visited Denver Seminary to explore the possibility of attending school in Colorado. Not sure of the next step he should take, he spent a day walking in the snow in the Rocky Mountains asking God to show him what to do next. Nothing happened—no grand revelation.

But later that evening, while watching TV in his hotel room and feeling depressed that God had not answered his question, he watch a news report on a school shooting in Arkansas. Images of student victims filled the screen gripping his attention:

> Something just struck me as I was sitting in my hotel room. We were really missing the boat on this. Everything I was doing in church wasn't affecting that world at all. We weren't permeating culture, and we weren't touching that stuff at all. We were just kind of hanging out playing our own games.

At 26 years old, Chris was overwhelmed with this realization. The images of the shooting moved him to ask questions about how to communicate and translate church in a way that people would respond to and understand. Chris recalls a passage of Scripture during the moment:

> The story of Zacchaeus in Luke 19 had jumped off the page and was haunting me. Christ had come for the outsiders and not the insiders. Everything I had been trained to do was about how to take care of the insiders. It destroyed me. That night, I went to God in prayer asking about what he wanted me to do, but I felt like his response to me was, 'Chris, what do you dream about? What kind of church do you dream about?' I wept for hours. I started writing and writing [that evening], and out of that came a kind of vision statement that is actually in our church today from that experience back in 1998.

Chris returned home and shared his experience with Nicki. Though he did not fully understand what had occurred, he knew something was birthed inside of him that night in Denver.

WHO TOLD YOU TO BE SUCCESSFUL?

Eventually, the Marshalls moved to Wilmore, Kentucky, and Chris enrolled in Asbury Seminary. Part of the decision to attend Asbury was its proximity to Cincinnati—just a two-hour drive from Wilmore. They fell in love with this city and had a heart to be right in the middle of it. They secretly longed to live in Cincinnati, but told no one of this desire.

> When I would drive through Cincy late at night, I would weep over the city and just pray for its people. I guess I was growing a heart for its people. When I would dream about my future, it was always in the context of Cincinnati. That has only deepened. I want to spend the rest of my life here and ask for God's kingdom to come.

Chris ended up spending three days a week at Asbury and would go back to Cincinnati for the other four days. Chris recounts another turning point during his time in seminary at Asbury:

> My next conversion happened during my first semester in seminary. Viv Grigg, a missionary from New Zealand, was a guest speaker. He was there to 'beg for our lives,' to consider walking among the poor in Calcutta. This guy was talking a whole different gospel than what I had heard. At the end of his talk, he just looked at all of us and said, "For you American pastors I have one more question. Who told you to be successful?" And then he turned around and sat down. I sat in my pew and couldn't move. He had completely undressed me with one question. I literally had nothing left. I guess I realized that, in fact, I'm not sure that all along I was even doing ministry. I was just trying to be successful. I know I cared about ministry and I cared about people, but I realized I was on real sinking sand—needing to be needed, all those kind of things. At that moment, I had to die to my addiction to success, and I realized most of what I had learned in the church growth realm was really how to be more and more successful. That was a real deconstructing moment for me.

The seminary exposed Chris to different perspectives of the Christian experience. George Hunter was a professor at Asbury, and Chris found himself reading the early manuscripts of Hunter's *Celtic Way of Evangelism*.[1] In the process, Chris discovered an attraction to Saint Patrick and Celtic Christianity. Not only was this due to his own Irish heritage, but he was also struck by the way Patrick went about "or-

1. Hunter, *The Celtic Way of Evangelism*.

ganizing" the church into clans. The European model revolved around building a cathedral in the middle of town to which all the roads led. In contrast, instead of starting with a centralized location of ministry requiring people to come and receive readymade spiritual goods and services, the first thing Patrick would do was to fall in love with the people. Only then would he communicate the gospel in ways people could understand. This Celtic approach of sharing Christ with others would have a profound influence on Chris and Nicki's ministry in the years that followed.

While studying for a Master of Divinity with an emphasis in evangelism and leadership development, the Marshalls attended the Vineyard Community church in Cincinnati, pastored by Steve Sjogren, a key leader in servant evangelism and author of *Conspiracy of Kindness*. It was a church of over 5,000 members when Chris became an intern under the direction of Jim Henderson (now with Off the Map in Seattle). During this time, Chris started asking missiological questions concerning the real nature of the gospel. Are there elements of the gospel that cannot change while other aspects of the gospel can change?

Up to this point in time, one thing that Chris and Nicki determined was that the best they had experienced in student ministry happened in their home—simply hanging out, showing hospitality, and building community. They realized that transformational ministry not only could happen in small intimate settings, but that these settings were most conducive for ministry. When Chris tried to program the ministry, it was a bad fit:

> Even though I could pull it off, I wasn't in my own skin. Some of what Jim Henderson was teaching me was that it was okay to be different. My heart, at this time, was completely for those outside the church. I had no desire to do anything within the church, but just plant these communities where the church was absent. If we were the first people ever to pull up on the shores of America today, if we didn't know anything known as church, what would you do? You can't tell me that you would go and try to spend all your money building a building. There's no way that would be where you would start. That's just a part of our assumptions.

While serving in various ministries at the Vineyard, Chris became familiar with Dieter Zander, who was using the term "micro-church" when considering transitions for the church in the future. Zander asked, "What if churches of the future were, in fact, not mega, but really small, and intentionally small, in order to produce the kind of authenticity that people thrive for?" For Chris, this was the paradigm shift that moved him away from trying to be successful, to simply trying to be authentic, genuine, and full of substance:

> That was a huge shift for me. It was almost like the last piece of the puzzle. Once I gave myself permission to think small and doable, I started to feel comfortable in my own skin. Even though my gifts were very much out front—teaching and entertaining, those kinds of things—that was not what I was feeling called to. It was not where I felt people would respond to the gospel.

Chris began dreaming what it would look like for a church to be made up of smaller communities that networked together:

> It wasn't a new idea. I knew there was such thing as house churches in the past. You have the Acts model, and I was familiar with the Jesus People in Chicago. And I even read some of Carl George's stuff on the cell church movement, but even that felt very programmatic to me. It lacked a certain relational part to it. I had done the serendipity training small group stuff, but that was still a little bit more content-driven rather than being about community.

As the Marshalls approached the end of Chris's seminary journey in 2001, they realized that he would either take a job with the Vineyard in Cincinnati, something he really did not want to do, or they were going to become church planters. They wanted to plant the kind of church that no one else would plant, that no one they knew would even think of encouraging them to plant. From Chris's perspective at the time, the conversation about emerging church was in its infancy and generally not accepted by the church at large. But he and Nicki were determined to church plant in a non-traditional way.

After graduating from seminary, Chris continued his involvement in several ministries at the Vineyard in Cincinnati. He had hoped to see a transition toward more missional ways of doing things, but it did not work out that way. What he did see was how much time and energy it took just to "put on the show." His discontentment continued to mount and ministry burnout began to take its toll. Chris was more convinced than ever that it was time to seriously think about church planting.

THE CALL TO PLANT SIMPLE CHURCHES

Chris began exploring online looking for opportunities and came across an ad looking for a "postmodern" church planter at Penn State. The sponsoring group was the Mideast Baptist Conference (MBC). Being from Philadelphia; he thought that this might be the right situation because of the terminology used to describe the position. In spite of this promising opportunity, Chris and Nicki had a growing burden for Cincinnati. Nevertheless, they felt impressed to inquire about the position, so Chris contacted the MBC. The director of church planting at that time was Dan Peterson. After some initial formalities, Dan said they were interested in the Marshalls, but he was not sure that MBC wanted them to go to Penn State. Dan asked, "We've been praying for Cincinnati for 10 years, so would you consider staying there and planting a church?" This was the first sign for Chris that they were supposed to belong to this family of people—he had never mentioned to Dan that they wanted to stay in Cincinnati.

Chris and Dan began meeting on a regular basis, and Chris laid out his plan as to how he envisioned church planting. He wanted to be very honest with Dan about his disenchantment with church-as-usual:

> I wanted to give Dan every option in the world to get out and say this in not possible or this is not what we do. The whole idea was to organize ourselves only in small communities without ever having a desire to launch a service on a Sunday. So there's no special time and there's no special place. And I wasn't even sure what my role would be. At that time, I didn't know if I would be supported full-time to plant these churches, or if I was going to go get a job and figure it out from there.

In March of 2001, the Marshalls began an evaluation process as church planters with MBC. This required a 4-day assessment and testing with other potential church planters. He remembers how some people on the assessment team had difficulty with his perspective, unable or unwilling to conceive of something different. Chris recalls the experience:

> The team of assessors totaled about twelve. Only with one of them did we have an ongoing relationship who knew us and our heart and vision. That final meeting [the day of the decision] was with him and one other who had converted to liking and trusting us, too. There was particularly one guy from California who told us emphatically, "It won't work". He said churches are built outside in, not inside out. You have to market to many [people]

and try to end up with a church in the end . . . not start with few and then grow into a church. I quickly realized that he wasn't wired relationally and I am, so that was the major difference between us. And I would say he would be right, if we wanted to be paid. But ours was a long-term, bi-vocational model where we had time to stay and live in the neighborhood and love people. It wasn't dependent on a timeline to have it all up and running at a certain date. . . . If you are unwilling to completely change the way you approach people, situations, and church with a different set of goals in mind, there is really no way for it to happen.

As part of the assessment process, Chris was required to address the group as if he were trying to recruit them to participate in a church plant. Since it was a "canned speech," he did so halfheartedly. Still unsure about this new direction, it was during this presentation that Nicki was captured by the idea and understood that this was what they were called to do. At the end of the assessment, the assessment team asked the Marshalls if there was anything they wanted to say before they shared their decision. Nicki turned and addressed the group, and said, "We are going to do this regardless of what you decide. Your only decision is if you are going to do it with us." The assessment team laughed in response, for they had already decided to lend support. Even the doubters had been won over to their vision!

Being "experimental," MBC had no unique ministry category for the Marshalls, so they placed them in the church plant category and gave him a grant for one year's support. This was not the typical three-year support plan commonly used in many church-planting ventures. Additionally, it would be difficult because finding people to support them in this different approach would be a major challenge. They also had two children at this time and a third on the way. With only a ministry degree, Chris had to find a way to support his family. There was an expectation that he would seek secular employment to supplement and eventually replace his support. But this expectation was basically his idea and plan, not pressure from MBC. MBC had little experience with bi-vocational models. Chris believes they were probably concerned for his family. But they decided to put their trust in Chris and sensed the passion for what he wanted to do. So with MBC's one-year grant, the Marshall's decided to move forward. MBC would also provide opportunities for them to speak at churches within the state of Ohio to share their story and raise support from local congregations:

They were very simple conservative people, but were very open. They appreciated church planting and they kind of saw us as missionaries, but they didn't understand us. So I had to do some work communicating in a way as to not put a barrier between them and us, and to really talk about the things we had in common. But every one of these churches really cared about missions and about being missional. And so I spoke in that language. These very simple, conservative churches came alongside and supported us!

ORDINARY COMMUNITY CHURCH

In April of 2001, the Marshalls purchased a home in Cincinnati, but they were not strangers to this city. Nicki grew up in Cincinnati and Chris lived there during high school, so they had roots established and social connections from which to build their core group. Chris also made connections when he was commuting to Cincinnati for work and attending seminary at the same time. Chris remembers:

> We spent about four days a week at Asbury for me to do school full-time and had a three day weekend in Cincinnati pretty much my entire three years doing the [Master of Divinity program] at Asbury. In fact, my final year we stopped renting a home at Asbury and I just rented a dorm room to commute there three days a week by myself as my family stayed in Cincinnati full-time at my in-laws'.

May 2001 marked the first meeting of "Ordinary Community Church." It was comprised of eight people they knew from their social network, people willing to think differently, people who shared similar experiences and feelings. Most were under forty years of age, white middle-class suburbanites, and college-educated professionals. It was comprised of ex-church and disenfranchised members along with non-church goers. Some in their group felt ostracized by the traditional church and were disillusioned by the shortcomings of church-as-usual. But even with the hope of starting something new, the early days of Ordinary Community Church were difficult and painful.

Chris was unemployed for a short time while living off the small one-year grant. They also had the feeling that much of what they did was questioned from some of their friends...his home church in Cincinnati and also the previous church where he had been a full-time staff member. Even some people commenting on his blog were critical of their approach to church planting. Under this pressure, Chris was tempted to go back to a ministry staff position that provided a full salary because of the difficulties they faced. He was journaling and explaining to God that if he [God] didn't come through, there was no coming through. There was no plan B. If this was going to be the church that he dreamed about, then this was it—no going back to ministry as usual.

Not long after their new journey began, this small group had the opportunity to learn some significant things about community. Chris recalls:

> We were all kind of detoxing together—very energizing. It was a little bit of us against the world. The only one in our corner was the MBC group. Dan and his wife would come down to visit, and they enjoyed our times together and confirmed our belief that this was of God. There is no question that our friendship together [with Dan and his wife] was the bridge to seeing this happen.

Their goal in the formative days of Ordinary Community Church was to introduce reproductive DNA in the life of their small community and set a missional example for future house churches and faith communities. Chris recalls, "Our focus was simply loving the people around us and being in conversations, trying to think more holistically about it—not much formal outreach." This relational mindset led to outreach in the form of backyard barbecues almost every week. It was like an "open party." They were learning how to do community in the suburbs. As a result, by Easter of 2002 they started a second house church. Chris reflects on this process:

> We started with one, became two within a year. Since then, we have started at least five others. Presently, there are four house churches meeting [as of April 2009]. Some churches, like all living things, naturally dissolve due to numerous re-locations of members to other cities. Or, in the case of the student house churches, they graduate and go off to college. We've had one house church discontinue due to a lack of leadership and another break off to form its own network in another area.

In their third year, Dan asked Chris to put a "structure" together about who they were as a church, what they believed, but to do it in their own unique way and style. So in May of 2004, MBC recognized their ministry as an established church, not just a church plant, even though they had no Sunday service, no building, and no paid staff. MBC created a new category for church planting within the district's church planting movement called Apostolic Church Planting:

> We really liked that name! We felt very kindred with the MBC because of the fact that they would think outside the box with us and care to know us and learn from us. And Dan was out there trying to recruit church planters and was running into all kinds of young men and women talking this way. So he started to help the district by assessing these new pioneering church planters of similar ilk. I think in the future there's going to be more of a role for me within the church planting movement of our district and of our larger conference to help in that way.

But the partnership was not without difficulties. There were obstacles created by expectations placed upon Chris based on how church planting had been done in the past. For example, he was asked to fill out church planting forms every month. He just stopped filling them out because they were not germane to what they were doing or to their understanding of mission. They did not have Sunday school attendance to count or a definitive number as to how many were in Sunday morning services. It simply did not apply to their situation. Their ministry focus was purely relational . . . families getting together in their homes for fellowship, mutual support in all aspects of life, and for rallying together in ways to touch their friends, associates, and neighbors with the love of Christ. The ministry of their small faith communities was not "programmed," but embraced as a way of sharing life together. So, early on when Chris was more insecure about their church planting efforts, the required reports that were designed for conventional church planters made the process more difficult, stirring up self-doubt and the feeling that no one really understood them.

But more recently, Chris describes the last couple of years as being "fantastic" with an overall sense of being matured as a community of faith:

> Community is not a buzzword anymore. It is truly how we have organized our lives. We belong to this group of people, we live life-on-life with this group of people, and the kind of evangelism we are doing is very missional, very ordinary and everyday, outwardly focused toward the people that we work with, asking God for his kingdom to come in all these situations that we are a part of. This fact has become more and more natural, and it's just been fun seeing that happen.

Chris found employment teaching Bible classes at a Christian school. It was difficult at times because of his unique perspective on church and the kingdom of God. He was talking about the gospel in terms of the kingdom of God in a place where the established church wanted a very safe subculture of Christianity. It was during this time that they started a house church for students—kids with nowhere to go. Some were into the homosexual lifestyle, others into alternative culture, a mixture of churched and unchurched youth—all meeting together in their home in the suburbs. The Marshalls simply talked to them about the kingdom of God and what Jesus had taught his followers.

In 2006, another student house church was started, a group of about twenty people meeting together on Sunday nights. Scriptures serve as a platform for discussion around topics such as the kingdom of God, prayer and worship, and communion is shared every time they meet. The Marshalls understand many students they work with are around only for a short season due to students' returning to college or finding employment:

> Our understanding of house churches is that they are very organic. It's just like planting flowers. Some of them are perennials—always there, always growing. And then some of them are annuals—you plant them for a time, they serve their purpose, they are beautiful in their season, and they go away. A few years ago, I had a couple of house church communities that were mostly high school teens who had no place to be. We started them a few times, and then they would graduate and go off to college. I've even married a few of them now. I was kind of the only pastoral presence that they had in their lives.

Another outreach into the community has been through hosting marriage seminars in their home during the summer months. Though scripturally based, they were trying not to be "too preachy." An invitation is given to friends to meet for six weeks for some friendly socializing and to talk about marriage. At the end of each six-week session, at least one or two families indicated interest in continuing to meet in some way. Chris reflects on their development as a faith community in building relationships with their neighbors:

> We've seen some really cool organic relationships happen in very natural ways for the kingdom to be proclaimed. We feel so strongly that we need to do more things to go public with procla-

mation without creating a system and programs, to do so in very simple ways. And whatever we do public has to serve whatever is happening in the communities—where relationship and transformation is happening—and not the other way around.

Another example of community ministry was conceived and implemented by a married couple from their network. They started a pre-teen house church for 4th to 8th graders in the same neighborhood where the Marshalls live. This pre-teen group includes about six or seven kids from participating families in their house churches. About twenty kids simply walk down to their house and "hang out." They get involved in Bible studies, outreach, collecting money and looking for ways to give it away. Over half the kids in the group are from different church backgrounds or have no church background at all. Recently, one of Chris's friends got involved in building water systems for villages in Africa. He attended the pre-teen house church and spoke to them about issues of water, poverty, and AIDS in Africa, and they learned that they could build a well for about $1,000. So they started a "well fund," as the kids called it. They started pooling together their allowances, and then had a garage sale and a small carnival where they raised $750 and continued to raise more money. This was all their idea and initiative. Chris comments with astonishment:

> I hear my kids all the time when we give them their allowance. They say this portion goes to the well fund—that's just all them. It's pretty neat. That may be one of our healthiest house churches [Chris laughs]! They simply get it, you know, they are committed—they get together. It's really neat to see them run with it. But one of my favorite scenes is to see these kids in their slippers come out of their houses on Sunday morning and walk down to this other home. It's kind of a cool thing.

Two adults are present with the kids—the couple that hosts the meeting in their home. Their goal is to empower the kids to take leadership and ask them what the group wants to do and then help them organize around their ideas. "We'll continue to experiment and grow with them to see what it looks like for them to host their own community and do community in a way that is appropriate for their age group and to think missionally about their friends."

In the fall of 2007, the Marshalls planted a new faith community that was the result of prayer and dependency on God to make it happen.

It wasn't rocket science, actually. It was a result of a simple prayer. Without question, my best contribution to the community is in starting new groups. One day I was driving to work and expressed a desire, 'God, I'd really love to start another community. And if there is anyone out there that you know'—I'm talking to God, so of course he knows—but it was really as simple as that.

Within a few days, Chris received several emails from different people who were at different places in their journey. They discovered Ordinary Community Church while doing online searches for house churches in Cincinnati. A new community of faith was birthed. "One of the couples is moving to the same eastern suburb where the other couples live with the desire for continuing the existing community and just figuring out ways to love their neighbors," Chris notes. The community teaches and emphasizes the importance of paying attention to the needs of their neighborhood.

GETTING OVER THE FRUSTRATION

Even though the Marshalls and Ordinary Community Church were connected with MBC and had Dan's support, there was still a sense of being alone, especially early on. But they began to meet other people in the region who were doing something similar. About one year into their work, Kevin Rains called him out of the blue.[2] Kevin had a friend in New Zealand who found Chris's website, and told him he should look him up. They lived just fifteen minutes from each other, but Rain's friend in New Zealand brought them together. Chris and Kevin struck up a friendship and began meeting together on a weekly basis. Very organically and naturally, they started having get-togethers with a small group of church planters in the area who were walking a similar path. "It was like a house church for me," Chris recalls. "We began to form this language [concerning the perception] that you are not alone. All of us had experienced a ton of pain in being alone. And we determined together that no one would ever be alone again."

Then tragedy struck during this time when their regional church planting group was taking shape. When two of their friends died who were vital members of the group, it was a galvanizing event. "We're not just hanging out here. We're in a spiritual war and we need each other.

2. For more about Kevin Rains and a community of house churches in the Cincinnati area associated with Vineyard USA, go to http://www.vineyardcentral.com.

We need to keep going, figure out how to reach people and love our neighbors." Not only did these tragedies galvanize their commit to one another, in the midst of their loss they found a global source of comfort and strength. Blogs not only connected them to each other, but the world as well. Thousands followed their stories all over the globe. "What we do in the local context is only part of what we do in our ministries," Chris comments.

"When we started out, we were probably a little bit more revolutionary. Now, we are a little bit more mellow. We just want to think more in kingdom terms. Being angry at the church is not a big enough idea. We want to see the kingdom come on earth as it is in heaven. That is a bigger idea."

Chris believes complaining about the failures of the traditional church is not worth the time and effort. For example, his attitude changed early on concerning conversations surrounding the topics of postmodernity and the "emerging church."[3] He began to see that the discussion was often more reactive against the church rather than being about Christ and his teachings. The postmodern "lingo" was a sign of elitism and being "cool." It appeared to him as mostly talk and filing complaints against the church, instead of actually doing something in constructive and positive ways:

> I made a decision that the people that I hang around with had to be doers. I already have to work a full-time job, have to figure out the next thing we are doing in this story of ministry, and didn't have a lot of extra time to just be involved in all these online conversations, or readying the next book on this or that. But I really wanted to be where people were. I just felt tired from all the talk ad nauseam about postmodernity. It was just talk. Did anyone actually want to enter into the lives where people were? That's where I wanted to spend my time.

Q & A WITH CHRIS MARSHALL

The following question and answer session with Chris is intended to give the reader more insight into his philosophy of ministry and to address par-

---

3. The term "emerging church" is understood by some as a protest against and conversation with the institutional church, arguing for the need to communicate in culturally relevant ways to a new generation that misinterprets or rejects forms and thought so prevalent in traditional churches.

ticular issues related to the topic of planting simple churches in partnership with denominational agencies and churches. Interviews were conducted between June of 2006 and April of 2009. Chronological references in the following interview fall within this time frame. As of June 2011, Chris continues to head the leadership team of Ordinary Community Church.

Rick: What is your understanding about faith and ministry in a postmodern culture?

Chris: Though I resonate with some of it, ultimately, postmodernity is not a satisfying worldview. It ends in chaos. It leads to such disillusionment that, theologically, I know people will not be satisfied. They will still be thirsty. There's no question that the kingdom is the only place where the heart is home.

Rick: What about church leadership? How do people understand your role in your faith community?

Chris: Early on, our ideal was that leadership structure should be completely flat, but then learned that this doesn't work. I used to be very apologetic with being a pastor, but now I'm very comfortable with that role. I'm more of a co-pastor with another couple. We have a leadership team that acts as an eldership. We always eat together once a month and talk about the overall spiritual issues of the community. People see me in that way, not real formal though. In times of crisis people look to me pastorally. I set some of the vision, but it's very shared, and I don't do everything. They call me "Pastor Chris" mostly when kidding around, but in reality they give me that role in their life. This is earned. And I'm ministered to as well when we gather and live life together. I call it permission leadership. They give me permission to lead them, and I definitely have to earn that permission.

Rick: What term would you use to describe Ordinary Community Church?

Chris: My favorite term is a missional community. But that's a term that will never take off because it's too hard to say. It actually explains, at least in my heart, what I believe it is that we do. I think the church universally has always had two things—it's always had the command to be missional in this world and in our neighborhoods, and that it functions best as a community. It's through being the people of God that we actually transform into being the people of God.

Rick: Has the composition of your simple churches today changed from your early days? If so, how?

Chris: The composition has changed in terms of nine years ago. We had [fewer] kids and they were all under seven [years of age] or so. Now we have over forty [kids] and there is a much wider span of ages. From a spiritual perspective, we have certainly attracted more disenfranchised folk, but have more contacts with non-churchgoers as well.

Rick: How effective were the first groups or house churches in reaching and ministering to the uninitiated, the outsider, the non-churchgoer, and the normal person across the street who has no interest in the organized church?

Chris: I would say we have been effective in being faithful to the relationships in front of us, and the neighbors we live in community with to serve. I observe that our members are hosting barbecues on their streets, throwing open parties, and are intentional about being in relationship with their neighbors. There are book clubs, Bible studies, barbecues, ballgames, social parties, family retreats, etc., to which [the] un-churched are coming and feel welcomed. There is a whole layer of people participating with the community at this level, but who haven't yet begun attending house church meetings. It is through these relationships over time, where they begin to ask questions about the larger [faith] community and how they can be more involved. We try to let the relationships happen organically and naturally, but the intentionality of our hearts is to reach out to our neighbors and be the embodiment of the kingdom in all circumstances. And as I reflect on the Sermon on the Mount, Jesus seemed to care most about the position of our hearts. I know that doesn't gel well with the American corporate and capitalist idea of productivity, but that's a whole other conversation.

Rick: What about missional effectiveness in recent years?

Chris: The communities I am working with today are doing this best at a relational level, like my bartender friend at the pub around the corner that I counsel with and take to AA; the pre-teen house church that has kids from the neighborhood that come out their doors in slippers to their [house] church, even though their parents won't go; and the women's monthly book club that typically ends up being subversive church meetings [where] ladies pour out their hearts in their joys and pains and get cared for. There are "unchurched" folk in all those kinds of interactions. As well, my wife and I host the neighborhood barbecue for our neighbors to promote community and the sharing of resources. We just think if Jesus lived on our street, he would initiate and host community. Of course, he'd also cook tasty food!

Rick: Do you believe there are characteristics of the church that transcend culture and historical context?

Chris: I see six aspects of the church when looking at Acts 2: they were a community; they had teaching based upon Scripture; they celebrated sacrament together, particularly communion and baptism; they worshiped and prayed together; they did outreach in the sense that they took care of the physical needs of people around them; and they were missional in that they desired to get this kingdom message out to the surrounding world.

Rick: Do you believe this simple way of doing and being the church is more conducive to facilitating the six characteristics that you just cited?

Chris: I think sometimes what it boils down to is the difference between more organic thinking and systems thinking. When you are thinking in terms of systems, you can get very institutional, whether you're mega- or micro-. But if you are thinking in terms of being a spiritual community, of being organic and that kind of fluidness, then you can be huge. But that's going to take the kind of leader that I may have not met yet personally. Is it possible? I guess I'm not going to rule it out. There may be some people who could navigate those waters better than I could. I'm not a CEO by personality. I do believe that we don't understand how much money controls what we do in the traditional ministry. We have no idea how much we think and talk about money. It should really be irrelevant. We don't need money to perform ministry. What we need are the people of God here on earth. I believe that money and those kinds of structures can become the tail that wags the dog.

Rick: What do you do with the idea that some house church proponents suggest that the New Testament pattern for the church is the
house church?

Chris: I'm not comfortable with making absolute that the only New
Testament church model is the house church. That's not the big
idea. The big idea was that the kingdom of God is the place where
you find the reign of God. And his rule is where people have a
desire to become his people. To me, in any context where this is
happening, this is where you find the church. The model of what
I'm doing is an expression of the church that I've come to love and
where I really feel at home.

Rick: What are the core values that you hold as a community of
faith?

Chris: We have four core values: community, authenticity, passion,
and mission. So for us, community and mission are the two univer-
sals that the church ought to be in every single culture. Authenticity
for us is a bit of trying to explain ourselves in this particular culture
where the church has lost its authenticity. Passion, as well, in that
we have made Christianity a thought or a belief, instead of a life
that is really meant to be lived. Authenticity can change with context, even the idea of passion, but community and mission cannot.

Rick: Do you have a particular ministry strategy that you adhere to
as a faith community?

Chris: I don't tend to think of what we do in terms of strategy.
Fundamentally, we believe that churches are born out of people
who make daily decisions to follow Jesus. As we seek the kingdom
together, God builds a church. So we don't focus on strategies like
in a business sense—rather, we focus on submitting to God and
letting him lead us. Our strategy is to love God, love one another,
and love our neighbors as ourselves. I know it's a cliché, but it's
our reality. We just try to give away what God gives us. It's a more
organic and relational approach and we're in it for the long haul.
We don't have a short-term business model with preconceived expectations of what the product needs to look like. We try to follow
God where he leads.

Rick: What kinds of relationships and networks do you seek to develop?

Chris: Our network of friendships with other house church networks continues to grow and strengthen. They understand us and we understand them. It provides mutual encouragement and resourcing. Because we operate at a zero budget—we give away 100% of our tithing income—then our partnerships are almost completely relational in their dynamic.

Rick: Do you still have the same convictions and passion that you did several years ago?

Chris: Yes, and that much more so. In some ways you might say that my edges have rounded. When we started seven or eight years ago, I had been hurt from some of my church experiences. Those wounds were probably still open, but there's definitely been some healing for me in the big picture sense. Whereas now for me, it's not simple church versus traditional church, or any of that stuff. I'll be friends with anybody who wants to do the kingdom—anybody, anywhere. In fact, I'm pretty critical of people my age and younger, within what some call the emerging church, that speak this kind of language. I'll be the first to critique it and say it's not an us/them thing. It's war out there, and we need friends. Anybody who wants to try something for the kingdom, I'm all for it. Whatever you want to attempt—let's do it.

Rick: What is your relationship like now [seven years later] with MBC?

Chris: It's somewhat distant now, but healthy. They don't need much from us now in terms of reporting back to them. I have conversations with the area pastor a few times a year and receive email updates from him once a month. We are not real active in denominational meetings, though I try to attend when my schedule allows. We are also quite a distance away from the concentration of churches that are part of the conference.

Rick: Do you still see yourself connected to the conference? Do you still see value in the relationship?

Chris: I do. There's certainly no reason not to. They've not come to us with a top-down approach. Because there was no money coming

from them, we could define our relationship as friendship and support. As the culture and attitudes about church planting continue to
change, I would like to be a resource for them, being able to return
the favor to them as they helped me get started. The key for both sides
of the relationship is simple humility. It's not about being right or
wrong. It's admitting this is really hard, it's war, and ministry is very
hard, so we need each other. Let's figure out our common ground
and cheer each other on. Life is too short to do otherwise.

AUTHOR'S REFLECTION

Church Nearsightedness

It's very easy to become preoccupied with our small ideas—ideas that
coddle and protect our personal biases and preferences about the church
and its purpose in the world (this is true of just about everything we
conceive). Sometimes our small ideas lead to denominational turf wars,
or to emotional and irrational justifications for our faith traditions, ministries, and church movements. The danger is that we can end up more
committed to institutional survival than to growing and demonstrating
the reality of the kingdom. When we take our eyes off "the" kingdom we
end up looking crossed-eyed at our own little kingdoms. This re-shifting
of focus from the kingdom to kingdoms degenerates into "church nearsightedness." (Alternative terms are "myopic ecclesiology" and "ecclesial
narrow-mindedness"—take your pick.) Church nearsightedness is similar to the condition of not being able to see the forest for the trees—denominational trees in this case. Our love for a particular kind of church,
ministry, denomination, etc., stands in our way of seeing beyond to the
greater kingdom of God. Sadly, this preoccupation often becomes more
a matter of marketing a brand name rather than His name. Fortunately,
prescription lenses are available to correct church nearsightedness:
Spirit-spectacles.

Being fitted with the spectacles of the Spirit not only enables us to
distinguish the forest of the kingdom from the denominational trees, it
also inspires us and quickens our faith by enabling us to see the wondrous
and mighty works of God (see Acts 2:11). When we start to view the
world from a kingdom perspective, we see the spectacles of the Spirit on
display everywhere we turn our gaze. The Spirit's activity is not confined

to any one of our little kingdoms. When we actually see this reality and embrace this fact with enthusiasm, then we can begin to demonstrate a unified effort to those on the other side of the street, and perhaps lessen their distrust and distaste for us. Then they will see by our familial love that the way of the kingdom is more important to us than the glory and success of our little kingdoms and small ideas (see John 13:35).

Driving Motivations to Cross the Street

It might serve us well to understand some of the reasons for the frustration and disillusionment that many simple church planters struggle with concerning church-as-usual. Some of their reasons for concern are justifiable, in my opinion. But again, these reasons should never be presented in ways that cause division.[4] Hopefully, I have not done so here.

Let's look at two reasons for their concern. These two reasons serve as driving motivations for street crossers (there are more, but these two are the most common). The first reason is the apparent inequity between the resources required to maintain the programs and structures of the institutional church and the ministry for which it exists. It is their conclusion that inordinate amounts of time, manpower, and financial resources are invested into programs, payrolls, and plaster. The priorities of the institutional church have largely been focused on maintenance rather than mission. This is extremely frustrating for people who feel called to take the gospel to the world around them. Could they be correct in their assessment, at least in some cases? If their assessment is accurate, is it not incumbent on those of us in traditional churches to make sure our resources are being utilized efficiently and effectively? This question should not to be taken as a criticism of the traditional church. It is simply an honest and sobering question intended to raise discussion about accountability with what God has given to the followers of Jesus.

This leads to a second driving motivation for street crossers. They are convinced that those who choose to follow Jesus are called to follow him into the marketplace. It is a call to go. They believe that significant num-

4. One can argue the point that it is sometimes necessary to make critical assessments that may end in church people choosing to go their separate ways. Right or wrong, church history is full of such examples. But we need not go out of our way to cause such separation. Divorce has a life of its own and will continue to sway many of us. Therefore, I humbly suggest that we go the extra mile and avoid divorce, and err on the side of caution and unity for the sake of our testimony to the world. It is the greater call and challenge of love to stay together and work out our differences.

bers of people exist in our multicultural and pluralist society who are not interested in church-as-usual. The people they desire to reach are resistant to organized religion and skeptical about a kind of Christianity that seems preoccupied with power, influence, and even politics. And they believe, no matter how hard we try to attract them into our church buildings, most of these people are going to ignore or reject the invitation. That's why simple church planters—street crossers—believe so strongly in taking the church to the people, to live out the culture of the kingdom in the midst of surrounding cultures that make up our individual neighborhoods, villages, towns, and cities. Street crossers believe the gospel needs to be expressed in everyday life in ways that make sense to people who are not interested in attending church on our side of the street.

Confessions of a Former IC Basher

It's true. I was once an IC (institutional church) basher. Since my interview with Chris, when I reflect on what the Marshalls and Ordinary Community Church believe is the bigger idea, I have to sit down. Sometimes I hang my head in grief—sometimes in tears. "Being angry at the church is not a big enough idea," Chris says. Too often we find ourselves arguing about who has a bigger and better idea, especially when it comes to the church and the way we think things ought to be. I should know. I used to start some of the arguments and identified with those who were upset and disillusioned with the institutional church. As a former IC basher, it was my opinion the traditional church just had it wrong, and it was my duty to point out the inadequacies and shortcomings of churches shaped by institutionalism. In the process, I have concluded that constructive criticism is *usually* a good thing, but divisive criticism is *always* a bad thing.

When it comes to church planting and starting new ministries—church plants of all shapes and colors—these new ventures are sometimes motivated by an underlying frustration with the apparent failures of the established church. I have met many dissatisfied but well-intended Christians who were simply fed up with "church-as-usual." Sometimes they just leave the church altogether. Some choose to stay behind with swollen tongues from constantly biting them, while others open their mouths and freely share their frustration in ways that stir division and controversy. But whether you are a house church planter or a leader in a traditional church, it is an ever-present temptation to coddle and protect our ministries, desperately trying to justify why we do church the way we do. In the process, we lose sight of the bigger idea. What's the big idea, you might ask? Simply put . . . it's the King and his kingdom and nothing less. That's the big idea. Anything less is a small idea.

A Unifying Voice

A hopeful and pleasant discovery I made along the way in writing this book came from my interviews with street crossers and simple church planters such as the Marshalls. Though only a few of their stories are presented in the book, I had the fortunate opportunity to speak with many more street crossers. Some of them could relate with my journey in the traditional church and had experienced similar frustrations and disappointments in ministry as well. But one thing I can say about all of them—they are *not* IC bashers, at least not anymore. Amazingly, some never were to begin with. The simple church planters I interviewed agree that the cause of the kingdom outweighs any disagreements they have with a particular form and method of church. More important issues demand our attention. Wars over how we choose to worship are very low on their list of priorities, if on their list at all. Nowadays I couldn't agree more. But not long ago, I was ready to pick a fight over ecclesiology (our theology of the church) and argue which methods and structures were "more biblical." That's not to say there is no merit in looking to Scripture for insight as to what it looks like to be the *ecclesia*, the church of God, and to live out the culture of the kingdom. The Bible is certainly the place we must start our search for understanding our life together as followers of Christ.

But the voice heard coming from this new breed of simple church planters is very inspiring and hopeful. It's a unifying voice, not a divisive one. It's a voice of response to need, not of reaction to dissatisfaction. For example, when it comes to the "house church movement" and other alternative expressions of church life, I hear two voices—two distinct streams of logic for being and doing church in a simple manner. One stream springs up from a large reservoir of painful experiences, disappointments, disillusionments, and frustrations. At its very best, this stream begins from a sincere desire to "get it right," to base church life on biblical principles, on a New Testament example of church life that is defined as being simple and relational. But at its very worst, this stream produces a corrosive and divisive flow of criticism—contributing to a widening gap between brothers and sisters in Christ. This is one thing we do not need more of in the church at large—division. Furthermore, our witness to Christ and his kingdom is devalued. An on-looking skeptical world resists our message and invitations to come join us as a result of our inability as Christians to get along and play well with others within our own family.

The second stream I see in what we might call the house church movement is a stream that wells up from a desire to reach a world that is not interested in church-as-usual. It understands and acknowledges that many onlookers will not come. We must go to them. It is very pragmatic. Within this stream, questions are asked as to how can we "do church" in a way that will reach and transform people, people that would otherwise never step foot in a traditional church service. Surprisingly to me, many of the church planters in this stream have "stumbled" upon a simple church way of being the body of Christ across the street, almost by accident. For them, it is a matter of what is needed and what works. And though many of these street crossers would say their personal preference is a more simple way of being the church for a multitude of reasons, they would also say *it's not the only way.* They agree it's time for some of us to stop bashing the established church. It's time to stop revisiting and reliving our wounds, put bickering aside, and work together for the sake of Christ and the world. Whether you are a "house churcher" who has spent an inordinate amount of time being critical of the institutional church, or a "traditional churcher" who has harbored a suspicious attitude toward those in house churches, it's time to cut bait and start fishing . . . together.

Worship Wars or Washing Wounds?

Shortly after the riots of Los Angeles in 1992, America was shocked by a video capturing the image of law enforcement officers dragging a man from his car while beating and kicking him. Weeks later this man stood before the news cameras and addressed the nation. "Can't we all . . . just . . . get along?" It would almost seem that Rodney King was a prophet. We should heed his advice when it comes to trying to get along in the church. In light of trying to get along, Chris Marshall's statement that being angry at the church is not a big enough idea is right on target! But thinking our way is best and being critical of the way others go about church life misses the mark of trying to get along. Whether we are arguing over who has it right between traditional and alternative forms of church life, or over issues such as worship styles, is it really that important—our personal preference? Crossers should always be questioning their own motives. When personal preference stands between two people (or churches), it usually ends in misunderstanding, frustration, and ultimately a broken relationship. The idiom for this divide is called "talking at cross purposes." This refers to having what appear to be opposing goals, opinions, or points of view. Instead, we should talk *about* cross purposes . . . about our communion in the cross of Christ . . . about our common purpose of making our Lord and his kingdom known throughout the world. Talking about cross purposes with those who "do church" differently will lead to a greater appreciation for their difference, thereby creating trust instead of suspicion and the possibility of partnership in ministry. So which is of greater value—to satiate our personal worship preferences and sentimentalities, or to support and encourage others on both sides of the street? It seems to me we are called to be healers of wounds, not inflictors. We are called to wash wounds, not worsen them. We are called to serve others first, not serve ourselves. Sounds real spiritual, right? But let's not get caught up in what is spiritual and what is not. Let's just agree to practice servanthood with one another, no matter who the other may be. Practice may not make perfect, but it certainly can make permanent.

The uniform of one who serves, including street crossers and all who follow the Way, is a towel worn around the waist. Jesus started this fashion trend, a design originally conceived and worn in heavenly realms—where God the Father is totally given to the joy of the Son, and the Son is totally given to the joy of the Father. Each is consumed with the preference of the other. Let us follow their example by laying down our preferences, donning our towels, and considering others better than ourselves—in our faith communities as well as those across the street.

An Apology

To my brothers and sisters in Christ who identify with the traditional church: On behalf of myself and hopefully anyone who has demonstrated arrogance and pride in thinking that we simple-house-church-preferring folk have a better idea, that our way is more biblical than any other expression of the church, please forgive us.

FOR PERSONAL REFLECTION AND GROUP DISCUSSION

1. Dan Peterson and MBC played a very important role for the Marshalls through their support and encouragement, especially in the early stages of planting and establishing Ordinary Community Church. How easy or difficult would it be for your church or denominational church-planting agency to come alongside a couple like the Marshalls and lend your support? What would be the challenges of such an effort? Come up with a list of steps needed to partner with simple church planters.

2. Chris has a mantra: "Church is not some place you go to . . . it's a people you belong to." Do you agree with his statement? Why or why not? If you agree, do the priorities of your church reflect this value?

3. Reflect upon or discuss what it means to be committed to the kingdom of God.

4. Do local church and denominational agendas and priorities sometimes interfere with the ability to see the broader kingdom concerns in your town or city? If so, what can be done to become more kingdom-minded in ways that will be reflected in the ministry philosophy and methods of your faith community?

5. Chris said in the early days of starting their first house church, the core group went through a "detox" process. If you are part of a simple church or a house church, can you relate to this process? Consider Chris's comment that "being angry at the church is not a big enough idea." Is there any degree of disillusionment with or resentment toward the traditional or institutional church in your faith community? If so, in what ways is this beneficial or detrimental?

2

Simply There

AN UNSETTLING PARADOX

"I HAD A PRETTY standard conservative evangelical experience," says Jason Evans. Being raised as a Free Methodist in his youth, his mother's affiliation was with the Assemblies of God, and his father was raised in an ecumenical environment, having attended churches of numerous denominational persuasions, including the Assemblies of God, Free Methodist, Baptist, Lutheran, and Brethren. Perhaps not surprisingly, Jason came to faith in Christ as a child. As he grew older, he was exposed to a variety of denominational teachings and perspectives. But it was during his junior high school years that Jason began to participate in activities and consider perspectives that did not fit particularly well into his conservative Christian upbringing. A prime example of this was when he was introduced to punk rock. This exposure brought about an interest in the ideology surrounding punk rock culture in his hometown of San Diego. In time, Jason became a musician and started several bands. Even as his interest grew in punk rock music and culture, he remained involved in church life. After graduating from high school, Jason dabbled in a few college courses, but over the next several years he primarily focused his efforts on finding employment and pursuing his musical interests through managing and booking tours for budding underground bands.

At the age of twenty-two, Jason married his wife, Brooke, who also grew up in San Diego. It wasn't long after getting married that another friend of Jason's, a Southern Baptist youth pastor, persuaded them to get involved at his church, eventually hiring Jason as an administrator of operations in 1998. Shortly thereafter, he became the young adult pastor. Stepping into ministry for the first time, the learning curve was steep and fast.

Along with his duties as an administrator of operations and young adult pastor, Jason was also orchestrating events surrounding a building campaign. But he found himself surrounded by an unsettling paradox. Though employed as a pastor to oversee the young adult ministry and worship service, Jason was also involved with young people outside the physical walls of the church . . . and these young people were having radical experiences of faith! They had no formal connection with the church. "The radical faith experiences happened in the small groups which spun out of our 'culturally relevant' service. They were small groups, started by attendees, but they attracted others who did not attend our service for the most part," recalls Jason. He was increasingly perplexed by the ineffectiveness of reaching young adults through the programs endorsed by the church in contrast with the vibrant ministry occurring beyond his official job description and ministry.

To cap it off, this paradox was unfolding at the same time he was overseeing a massive building campaign. Jason began to question if the financial resources raised through a building campaign would be money well spent. Jason recalls some of his questions: "Are we spinning our wheels here? Is the system broken? Are we now saying that people can have a true spiritual experience that can be healthy and very holistic and does not rely at all upon the ecclesiastical system that we've cultivated here in the Western world?"

The theological dilemma brewing in Jason's mind led to his resignation from his position as a young adult pastor. Because he was in a position of leadership and holding to alternative views of ministry, Jason thought it was best to resign. It was as though he were asking all the wrong questions at the wrong time. No one was listening. He continued to participate at the church as a layperson in order to set up leadership for the young adult service before stepping away entirely from his church staff position. After his resignation, he found work with a marketing company, and eventually was employed as an operations manager for a construction services company.

CHURCH AT MATTHEW'S HOUSE

During this time of transition in 2001, Jason met three other pastors from a nearby seeker-friendly megachurch who had also resigned from their positions. They had a desire to do "something different," but had no idea know what that difference would be. Jason was drawn toward these former pastors. Eventually, Jason and Brooke met with them over dinner, sharing with one another their ideas and personal journeys, and what they felt God might be asking them to do. Jason recalls, "We were pretty much hooked. We really felt like something was happening in those conversations and we needed to stick around to find out." Jason and Brooke began to meet with these former pastors and their wives for meals on Thursday evenings. They would simply meet for fellowship and pray.

> At first, it was a matter of getting together to lick our own wounds. But we had to readjust to life. We didn't hold positions of authority and power that we used to have. We had to figure out our place in the world, since we were not going to be committed to this thing [traditional church structures] that we thought we would be committed to for the rest of our lives.

Near the end of 2001, Jason and Brooke came to the conclusion that they should start a church with people they knew who were curious about a new kind of church. At least that was their initial thinking. As they began to gather in a small group and pondered the idea of planting a church, talk about a "launch date" would come up in their discussions, but nothing ever came of it. As they continued to gather and meet in conversational settings—where dialogue and personal life stories and experiences were shared—they started to see dynamic changes in the lives of people, even in themselves. Jason and Brooke began to feel a greater sense of authenticity in their spiritual experience than they had in the past. This had never happened before, even as leaders at the church where Jason had been employed.

One particular night, someone brought a friend who immediately identified herself as an agnostic and not interested in Christianity. Dinner came and went. They gathered after the meal to quietly worship and pray—nothing sensational or spectacular. In the middle of that setting, the girl said, "God, I don't know who you are, and I barely know these people, but whatever they have, I want it." The rest of the group looked at each other as if to say, "Can she do that? Did we just hear what we think we heard?" This experience illustrates the nature of the gatherings they referred to as "Matthew's House."[1] They were committed to the idea behind the story of Jesus going to Matthew's house—where "sinners" were gathered together

1. For more information about the present status of Matthew's House, visit their website at http://matthewshouse.com.

at a table with Jesus and his disciples. Jason recalls, "We knew that's what we wanted to do. We wanted to create environments where sinners and saints could commune together, could learn from each other, where the lines of the sacred and the secular were blurred."

This threw the whole idea of a "launch date" out the window. With the launch date mentality, they had been thinking, "take 'church' and paint it postmodern." But they kept hitting roadblocks in their conversations about starting a church, such as the money and programming necessary to launch such a church. They found themselves asking if this is really what they wanted to do. These questions brought them back to some of the very reasons they had resigned from ministry in the institutionalized church in the first place. Their questioning resulted in a failure to launch.

On the other hand, the Matthew's House approach to church life captured their imaginations and began to fulfill their desires for something different and authentic. All their subsequent faith communities began the same way: an open invitation to anyone for dinner and conversation about spirituality. Typically, they started out by explaining their view on Christian spirituality and how they practiced it—including an explanation of and participation in the Lord's Supper "Most often, those who 'stick' are post-church people and non-churchgoing people. Every once in a while, we'll get folks that still attend church somewhere and we are comfortable with that."

Over the next several years, Jason and Brooke started six Matthew's House communities, with two surviving and remaining healthy. Jason explains:

> The early communities we established totaled about six. We intentionally shut two of those down because they were based too much on affinity rather than a sense of mission. One shut down because of marital strife amongst the leaders. One split up when all participants moved away. Subsequently, each of the five core couples either started or helped start new communities in their new cities. Of those early communities there are two that remain. The "composition" of the group is primarily former pastors and people with no previous church background. Odd, huh?

In addition to planting Matthew's House communities, they also befriended other small faith communities in the San Diego metropolitan area and would come together on a monthly basis for worship and sharing.

MOVING TO THE CITY WITH THE MENNONITES

In 2004, Jason and Brooke decided they wanted to be in an urban environment where they would continue to pursue this newly found way of
church life. After discussing this idea with the leaders of their network
of Matthew's House communities, it was confirmed that an urban context was where they needed to be. They sold their house in the suburbs
of San Diego and moved to South Park, an historic neighborhood at the
heart of San Diego. As they made this move, Jason and Brooke began
reading books from an Anabaptist perspective, including *The Politics of
Jesus* by John Howard Yoder, and *Resident Aliens* by Stanley Hauerwas and
William Willimon.[2] Anabaptist polity made sense to them in terms of how
Christians should function. It challenged the assumption that the popular
and traditional way is always the right way. Historically, Anabaptist tradition has questioned popular Christian thought and practice, and this
questioning of the status quo particularly resonated with Jason.

Their newfound interest in Anabaptist history and polity grew
deeper when they crossed paths with Jeff Wright. Jeff was the bishop
of the Pacific Southwest Conference of the Mennonite Church and the
president of its mission agency, Shalom Ministries. Shalom is a ministry
of the Mennonite Churches of Southern California and is the designated
home missions agency for the Pacific Southwest Mennonite Conference.
Shalom Ministries has several small ministry units, the most notable of
which is The Center for Anabaptist Leadership (CAL). Some refer to Jeff
as the "CAL guy." At the time when he met Jason and Brooke, he had
oversight of church planting, church coaching, peace and justice advo-
cacy, worship ministries, international partnerships, service ministries,
and theological education. He was also contracted by the conference as
their regional pastor, providing primary oversight to thirty-one congregations in the conference and eight "emerging" projects. Jeff recalls how
he first heard about Jason:

> I got an email from a guy who is part of the oldest Mennonite
> conference in the country. Here was this old, established, main-
> line, 250-year-old conference of churches that was trying to rep-
> licate systems and structures like we had [Center for Anabaptist
> Leadership] and we were looking at them thinking how nice it
> would be to have their kind of resources at our disposal. But my
> friend tells me I need to meet this guy, Jason Evans.

2. Yoder, *The Politics of Jesus* and Hauerwas and Willimon, *Resident Aliens*.

As Jeff considered a first meeting scenario with Jason, the possibility that he might come across as being far too bureaucratic and institutional for Jason concerned him. So he decided to ask another pastor to go in his place. A meeting was arranged. After returning from the meeting with Jason, the pastor excitedly reported back to Jeff. "We've got to partner with this guy, Jason Evans. This is the kind of guy who will bring new life and new vision to us. I don't know if we can help him a whole lot, but he can bring a lot to our table."

"So, Jason and I met," Jeff recounts. "Then my wife and I went down and met Jason and his wife, Brooke, and we've had this ongoing relationship since then and it's just been wonderful. He really has brought a whole new dimension of leadership and vision."

Jeff became a supportive friend and a valuable resource for Jason and Brooke during this time of transition to ministry in an urban context. The region that comprises the Pacific Southwest Conference is culturally diverse, urban, and includes a variety of refugee churches for displaced immigrants. Because of this diverse cultural mix, Jason sensed that this particular conference was a group of people who appreciated what he and Brook were attempting to do. As a relationship ensued with Jeff Wright and the conference as a whole, they also continued to maintain their relationship with the network of fellowships that sprung from Matthew's House. Jason recalls what he thought about this new relationship with the Mennonites: "I think initially, once we saw that they wanted to partner with us and saw us as legit, we wondered what kind of resources could come out of this." On the other hand, they were not headed toward any structures or systems that needed material assistance, so physical and financial resources were not of great concern at the time. But what was important to Jason and Brooke was far more significant than finding a financial backer: it was Anabaptist and Mennonite history, knowledge, wisdom, and experience that they wanted. They desired a relationship with the conference on a level that would allow them to learn about their values, traditions, and theology that would serve as a foundation for their own ministry. They were certainly committed to identifying with the Pacific Southwest Conference of the Mennonite Church label, but had yet to realize where they would fit into the whole denominational picture on a larger scale.

INTENTIONAL COMMUNITY AND MAKING CONNECTIONS

As their relationship with the conference began to take shape, Jason and Brooke had already moved to the urban area of San Diego as co-owners of a residential property with three living spaces. This is what Jason calls "intentional community." It began with Jason, Brooke, and their two children. In addition to their family, in a house on the same property behind them, lived another couple with their two children. Shortly thereafter, two young single men took up residency on the floor above Jason and Brooke. That number eventually grew to five. One of these men considered himself a "flaming atheist." He was not interested in God—"if anything, maybe Buddhism," Jason recalls. But this young man was intrigued with what they were doing and wanted to join their community. Jason told him, "We take Jesus pretty seriously here, so if you're cool with that and want to move in, that's fine." Not only did he decide to move in, he ended up participating in their home meetings for a length of time. Some two years later, he moved to the Bay area where his fiancée was going to school. As a Filipino-American, he was baptized as a Roman Catholic. He and his fiancée started to go back to church during Lent. He later told Jason, "I don't know about this Christendom thing, but I'm going to give Jesus a chance."

Jason, Brooke, and their small faith communities provide an excellent example of taking the gospel across the street, or, in this case, upstairs. Their move to an urban neighborhood surrounded them with opportunity. It also placed them right in the middle of a multicultural environment. With large Southeast Asian and African refugee populations close by, they began developing relationships among different people groups. For example, in 2004, Bantu refugees from Somalia received special assistance from the US government because of the persecution and strife these people endured. En masse, they began to immigrate to five major cities in America, including San Diego. At the same time, missionaries from different parts of the world came back to the US to minister to the Bantu because they were still considered an "unreached people group." Where these missionaries had plans to gather the Bantu into big gatherings to show the Jesus movie, Jason found himself wondering if this approach was appropriate, suggesting that perhaps there was a more natural way of sharing the gospel. He tried to initiate discussions with local ministry organizations that were attempting to evangelize the Bantu about what it might look like for there to be "Jesus mosques" in

San Diego, since these people were primarily animistic or Muslim. But his suggestion was not well received. Once again, it seemed as though Jason was asking the wrong questions at the wrong time.

Another example of connecting with people across the street came in 2006. Jason, Brooke, and one person from their Sunday night house church met with a very diverse group of local people, individuals outside of their faith community. The purpose of the meeting was to discuss the idea of starting community gardens and finding ways to eat and live healthy in San Diego. They committed to meet consistently for three months and then see what might happen next. At the end of the three months, most had decided to start community gardens. As Jason shared this experience with his faith community, he told them that they were sensing that a "church" would come out of this group of people. At the end of their three-month commitment, some in the community garden group were talking about continuing to meet for a few more weeks. One member of the group commented, "I come here every week and I think this is my church. I call this my organic Bible study when I tell people about it. This is where I get closest to God." Jason just looked at Brooke as if to say, "There you go—an organic Bible study." All they did was host the meeting. Their love of Christ and willingness to cross the street to connect with their neighbors heightened a spiritual hunger for community within the hearts of those who had first assembled together around the idea of a community garden.

But the story did not end there. Another member of the community garden group suggested how they could show gratitude during the mealtime they shared at each gathering. Everyone agreed with her, so every week they opened with what was essentially a prayer. They thanked the Creator for creating the food and for providing the hand that prepared it from the soil to the table. Gratitude was expressed for being part of a community and working together toward something positive. Yet Jason and Brooke made no overt proclamations of the gospel that resulted in bringing this about. It was in that place of sharing a common interest and concern that apparently created a safe and welcoming environment. It was also a setting where Jason, Brooke, and a fellow street crosser brought something of Christ to that place of common interest and concern, all accomplished without the need to force a discussion about the Bible or church-related topics. Had they done so, there would have been no interest from the outset in forming a "Bible study," per se. The

Bible and church were not issues of common interest or concern for this group of normal people. The key was to find an issue that was important to everyone in the group . . . a common starting point. This principle would serve as a key element in the process of establishing small communities of various kinds.

HOME IS WHERE THE KINGDOM IS

As a part of a learning process, Jason began to see a need beyond that of simply starting faith communities. Their attention was being drawn toward trying to participate in the kingdom by indentifying where it was being made known in the city—toward finding places of pain and injustice in their city and mounting a charge against that darkness. In doing so, they started what is called the "Commonwealth Forum." The forum addresses issues of importance to people of San Diego, especially in the urban center. In a Q&A type forum, experts with positive messages and services come together with the community to address pressing issues of mutual concern, such as racism and homelessness. Living in an urban setting that is increasingly being gentrified, Jason and Brooke have sought to cultivate relationships and build bridges with people around common causes. In the process, they have discovered that many of their newfound acquaintances have given up on the whole idea of Christianity. Jason explains:

> We tell them they can give up on Christendom, but we think Jesus was onto something, so give him a chance. And most of the people of our faith community will probably never set foot in a church again. Even more so, we've tried to see where the kingdom could be active and in areas that are even further distant by trying to get involved with our Muslim neighbors. We've gotten involved with groups starting gardens in poor neighborhoods that is cost-effective, healthy, and creates a sense of pride in their neighborhood.

In the last few years, people in the area started calling their faith community "Hawthorn House," because they live on Hawthorn Street. It's now part of a growing network of communities, similar to theirs, known as "The Ecclesia Collective."[3] It is comprised of people with whom they've been in relationship—new people they have met along

3. For more information about the Ecclesia Collective, visit their website at http://www.ecclesiacollective.org.

the way, others who were once part of their faith community, and people they have mentored and who have decided to start their own communities of faith. It has become an ecumenical network of Christians working together for the kingdom of God in the city of San Diego.

One of the groups Jason and Brooke met with consisted of Buddhists, a lesbian couple, and people interested in pagan rituals. This is not your run-of-the-mill conservative evangelical church group. "I don't know anymore if the majority of the things that we do would even be on anybody's radar," Jason notes. "The Mennonites have been incredibly kind to us, they love us, they pray for us, and they are encouraging. I don't know if they always understand, but they stand by us. They claim us as one of their own. That's been refreshing and a real blessing."

This sense of connection and acceptance by the Mennonites was affirmed even more when Jason was invited to an assembly of representatives of the churches that make up the conference. Along with several others from their urban fellowships, they met people who had only heard of their ministry, but told Jason they had been praying for them. This touched Jason and his team deeply. At times, they had felt they were all alone and that no one really cared or supported them aside from Jeff Wright. This opened their eyes to the bounty and blessing of people supporting their efforts in prayer. Jason remembers thinking, "Who are these people? They're awesome! Some of us couldn't be more different than each other. We were just hooked. We saw people that were really trying to take following Jesus seriously. And while our paradigms were really different, we couldn't deny that they were people we wanted to partner with."

Supporting his family and finding time for ministry has been a constant challenge for Jason. Until early in 2008, he was employed by the same construction company that had hired him after he resigned from his ministry position with the Southern Baptist church. But his faith community and a number of friends outside their network of simple churches encouraged him to consider going back into full-time ministry. In addition, his Mennonite family stepped in with assistance by offering Jason a part-time position as a consultant with The Center for Anabaptist Leadership.[4] Jason recalls:

---

4. For more information about The Center for Anabaptist Leadership and Shalom Ministries, visit http://urban-anabaptist.org/cal/index.php.

We kind of took a leap of faith and it's been [interesting]. It's been good. Our community really wasn't asking us to go back into ministry for their benefit. They weren't asking me to be their pastor. It was more of a recognition that there was a lot going on and a lot of things we were adding to the community in the city and in the neighborhood. It just made sense that Brooke and I free up our time to focus on those things. So, a handful of people have stepped up and started to support us.

Q &A WITH JASON EVANS

The following question and answer session with Jason Evans is intended to give the reader more insight into his philosophy of ministry and to address particular issues related to the topic of planting simple churches in partnership with denominational agencies and churches. Interviews were conducted between July of 2006 and October of 2008. Chronological references in the following interview fall within this time frame. As of June 2011, Jason continues his involvement with Hawthorn House and The Ecclesia Collective, and is presently Director of Outreach and Evangelism at First Presbyterian Church in San Diego.[5]

Rick: Tell me about your relationship with the Pacific Southwest Conference of the Mennonite Church.

Jason: They definitely have adopted us in the sense that they believe what we are doing is important for the institutional church to appreciate and learn from. We are not considered an official congregation of the conference. But I think that has a lot to do with the fluid nature and the fact that our community really doesn't fit into the typical boundaries of any denominational structure. We still have a healthy working relationship with them. They actually brought me on part-time at the Center for Anabaptist Leadership that is affiliated with the conference [teaching, speaking, training, and coaching]. It's fun and it's a challenge at the same time. Most of the people are from Anabaptist circles and from more of a standard church practice, so there's a bit of a disconnect in approach. But I think more and more people are realizing that things have certainly not been working the way they should for the last few decades, so there are people open to thinking about doing things differently.

5. Learn about First Presbyterian Church in San Diego at http://www.fpcsd.org.

Rick: If the conference doesn't look upon you as an official congregation, then what is their understanding or perception of who you
are?

Jason: That's a good question. I think kind of like a potential congregation [Jason chuckles]. They would consider us as a church
plant in utero—a developing church plant. It's a fluid box that the
conference leaders have developed for groups just like us, so we
can have a relationship and we can be in community with different
congregations and leadership. But at the same time, it doesn't force
us to be something that we are not.

Rick: Do you desire more from your relationship with the Mennonites?
Are there more ways that they could assist you, or ways you could
help the Mennonites?

Jason: In a perfect world, I have a lot of ideas that would be incredible
to see happen. But practically, I'm also content where we are. The
denomination doesn't have a lot of money and resources, and neither do we. So I understand that what we have, and a relationship
as friends and partners in kingdom stuff is pretty cool. I don't ever
want to take that for granted, just because of some lofty ideas. But
with that said, we've talked about different things, most of it being regional. It's a unique situation, because the Pacific Southwest
Conference is very missional. Just about everything they've done is
very foreign to Anabaptist tradition, at least when it's been in the
[USA] . . . I definitely want to learn more from them. They've been
in the city. And being in an urban environment, being Anabaptist,
and being missional, they really understand [the culture] and have
a lot of contacts. There is a richness of theology [and] I want to find
ways to disseminate that knowledge with the people we work with.
I would love to find ways for us to continue to show people, who
basically just sit in the pews, that this is typically where the journey
ends, but expose them to the fact that it's not necessarily where it
has to end. They have power and authority given unto them as well,
and they can step out and do some pretty radical things that they
choose to do.

Rick: What are the key characteristics in your understanding of the
body of Christ, of the church, that transcend history, or culture
context? Or can you do that?

Jason: First of all, I don't think you can. Part of our problem, especially in the Western context, we've assumed we can take Jesus outside of first-century Palestine and understand what he was talking about, and you just can't. You can't understand the magnitude of his actions and his words and his life, death and resurrection, without understanding him as a person that lived in first-century Palestine and deeply rooted in the story of God's people—the Jews. His story is fairly empty without understanding how it fits into the bigger picture of God. Or at least it will have a lot of holes in it and not be very potent. I think we need to return to his story and the story of Abraham, the whole story of Scripture to get a handle on what it is we are supposed to be today.

Rick: Let me put it this way. Let's say you were transported back to any point in history since the time of Christ, and you were to walk the streets of a particular community . . . what would it be, what would grab your attention, where you could say, "Hey look, I think I see the body of Christ?"

Jason: It would be whoever was developing an alternative community out of people who were mostly the least, the last, and the lost. They would be the people that were doing that as a deep-rooted, central call or mission inside of them. I'd look at those people and say, "There's the kingdom." I think that's where I would probably look first. This is my bias, but I certainly would be paying attention to people who questioned the establishment—not necessarily in revolt—but definitely people who questioned and were very interested in another way.

Rick: What do you mean by *alternative*?

Jason: *Alternative* has meaning on several levels—alternative to the mainstream culture, alternative as in a faith community being an alternative family. For most of the people in our community and the Matthew's House community, it's the first kind of healthy family they have been a part of—an alternative social group to the normal social groups they've experienced that are not healthy. It's an alternative as in not subscribing to the ways of popular thinking—the popular ideas of how things work socially, economically, and culturally. Because most often, it's the people with the least ammo—the least, the last, and the lost—that don't fit into those things. To be with and to embody the gospel to those people, you have to set those things aside anyhow.

Rick: How effective were your first groups in reaching and ministering to the uninitiated, the outsider, and the "normal" person across the street who has no interest in the organized church?

Jason: The first communities were fairly effective, by my estimation, in reaching out to people with no previous church background. Those groups, as well as those we currently are working with, have also done a good job at working with those who are disenfranchised with the church. This is a huge portion of the population. Most churches don't have people between 18 and 30, and that [age group] makes up the majority of our communities.

Rick: What do you do with all the terms such as *house church, simple, organic, emerging,* and *missional*? Do they mean anything to you?

Jason: I've avoided using them as much as possible. I don't think they matter to anybody but church leaders, to be honest with you. Most people who are not involved in that type of stuff, people who we work with, don't really care. So a few years ago I stopped using that kind of terminology because it didn't seem to matter. If you asked people in our community, "What is this?" they would say, "It's my church," or they might simply say, "It's my community." It's being with people where I express my spirituality. It probably depends on their background. The only title I really struggle with is this whole emerging church thing, just because it's been so commodified. It bothers me. It's not a sales pitch. It isn't for sale. It isn't a learned technique.

Rick: If you had to describe to church leaders what it is that you do, what would you say?

Jason: We are trying to cultivate environments where the kingdom is announced and displayed. As far as what that looks like, we meet in homes, so I guess you can call us a house church. It's a church that is pretty much indigenous because it's mostly comprised of San Diegans who were born and raised here. And we're starting new communities in San Diego, so I guess that makes us organic. We are missional in the sense that we are a mission that does not subscribe to the typical Christian culture. We are doing our best to find what we call the "bleeding edge of the kingdom"—to try to be as far out on the edge as we possibly can. A pastor friend of ours says that we try to do everything short of losing our salvation—you hold on with your pinky, just so you don't lose your salvation.

Rick: You and I had a conversation about two years ago when you mentioned that you had no need for systems and structures. Do you still feel this way?

Jason: This is what we are doing now full-time, but I still don't think we are moving into a place where we need to have infrastructure or buildings on a regular basis. I think we are actually at the stage now where we are talking with four or five different potential communities starting up within the next six months, and we are talking about what this looks like. Our hope is that it really does remain a decentralized cooperative, so that these communities co-own and decide what this collective is, what happens, and where it goes. So, I really don't think we are headed toward institutionalizing or developing the overhead and infrastructure. At this point I don't see how that could be necessary. If we were to go in that direction right now, and I had to say here is my reason why we should go in that direction, a lot of it has to do with the work we are doing with immigration. We've been working more and more with other people around the issue of immigration. It's taking a lot of effort and a lot of work, so that's why we need a secretary and an office space. But really what that does is just recreate the wheel and start isolating us from all the people whom we have to be interdependent with who are also working on the same thing. It's a common evangelical church tendency to do it on your own, put your name on it, have your own office for it, and not have a clue what anybody else in the region is doing about said cause or said concern or ministry in the community. But by being kind of a decentralized network and by choosing not to be completely self-reliant, but being interdependent with those who are also seeking the kingdom in San Diego—it looks healthier. It's much broader.

Rick: What does leadership mean to you?

Jason: Leadership is never assumed. It's given by the people. A true leader never assumes the role. It is recognized and given by people in a community. A true leader is like William Wallace who was the first guy to charge into battle. He wasn't up on a hill watching and commanding from afar. That's a spectator. Our duty as leaders is to be the first ones to stick our necks out there and risk our lives. And if people follow you, you're a leader.

Rick: Does the traditional, institutional church need to be reformed or changed? Can it be?

Jason: I think the system's broken. I don't know if it can be fixed. Constantine is dead. He's still the emperor of our imaginations and I don't know if there is any salvaging. There are examples and glimmers of hope here and there. I think there certainly could be a resurrection at some point, but it's got to die first. People say they want to reform the church, but they don't really appreciate what that really means. Reformation is bloody and ugly. There's so much at stake—from financial [issues] to authority and power. But I love the church. I would not have realigned myself with a denomination after leaving the institutional system if I did not love the church and want to participate in the lives of those people who are part of that system.

Rick: Do you see a difference in some of the house church movements of recent decades and what you see happening now?

Jason: I think the difference between the [older] house church type things and the more recent movement, is that we've been lurking inside of postmodernity for a while, and we've gotten a lot more comfortable with things. Things are a bit more fluid. We are not as interested in carving out our niches—this is clearly in this box and that's clearly in that box. I think the difference [in] the '70s and '80s, when there was a resurgence in those ideas, as opposed to now, is some of that [niche-carving]. While I think the system needs to die, I'm willing to participate in it, with denominations and evangelical friends of mine. Jesus is my Lord and I want to participate in the kingdom of God. That is where my allegiance is primarily. For example, while I think our political system is broken, I still participate in it and try to speak into it. I still vote and I'm okay with that. It has to do with the shifts in culture and being a lot more fluid with grace-space.

Rick: If you had the opportunity to address a group of traditional church leaders and simple church planters, what would you tell them?

Jason: I would restate the Great Commission. We have to take this whole love thing pretty seriously. Jesus said this was the crux of his whole message. It cost him his life. It cost most of his best friends their lives. And it was love. What kind of love is this? We really need to dig in on this and find out what find out what it means.

Rick: Are your heart and vision basically the same as when we spoke two years ago, simply following Christ in the midst of life and going wherever he leads?

Jason: The last four years I've been very intentional about trying to see where kingdom of God is already unfolding and trying to help move people in the direction of getting involved in that wherever it is. The only other thing I would add to that is that when we see the powers of darkness moving strongly, *we do our best to see that the kingdom of God gets a piece of the action.* We try to move into the middle of [the darkness] and be a blessing when we can to bring peace and justice where it is necessary. That's our agenda. We have a variety of assumptions around that agenda. For example, you can't make change without community, so we need to talk about things like community. We also can't make change and participate in things "community" unless you have an inward journey and understand spiritual formation. It's not like we're just running willy-nilly around the neighborhood looking for something to do. We are very strategic and we have a lot of forethought in the things we do. But we start by asking the question, "Where is the kingdom of God unfolding?" That's where we need to be. Just like the old adage: "Don't ask God to bless what you are doing, but bless what God is doing."

Rick: More than once during our conversations, you have used the expression, "the least, the last, and the lost." What do you mean by that expression?

Jason: Not only is that a conviction of mine, but that is where we see Jesus hanging out. Not only is it my conviction, but the overarching story of Scripture seems to speak of a God that gives preferential treatment for the least, the last, and the lost. I have always, even since a young age, been a sucker for the underdog. So that's just the way I am. I guess it's because I just take Jesus at his word when he said, "When you clothe them, you are clothing me. When you feed them, you are feeding me." Gosh, if participating in the lives of people like that means I get to participate with Christ, then why not?

Q & A WITH JEFF WRIGHT

The following question and answer session with Jeff Wright is intended to give the reader more insight into the reasons and mindset informing and motivating a denominational agency to support simple church planters. The interview was conducted in July of 2006.

Rick: Describe the ministry purpose and philosophy behind Shalom Ministries.

Jeff: It's kind of a soup-to-nuts equipping strategy. Our mission at Shalom Ministries is to equip leaders, to empower churches, to embrace God's mission. We call it the "E3 Strategy."

Rick: You mentioned that part of your role is to give oversight to "emerging" projects. What do you mean by the term "emerging?"

Jeff: Emerging means anyone whom we have a relationship with who has not joined us in a formal or legal way. In Jason's situation, we basically adopted something that was already existing. We built a relationship together and our conference decided to put their arms around what Jason was doing and said, "Yep, that's us. We like that." Each of our emerging projects varies in terms of its relationship to the conference. Some have a strong and connected relationship; some have less of one but more of an identification piece. All of them, though, go through some training requirements that we have.

Rick: What is your motivation for having these emerging projects if they are not officially Mennonite?

Jeff: The harvest is plentiful and the laborers are few. We're not in the business to simply plant more Mennonite congregations, or have more Mennonite brand name out there. We do okay with that, but if something emerges and doesn't stay Mennonite, that's okay. God has a place for it and we'll celebrate that and move on to the next thing. We're just wanting to see kingdom ministry happen, and if it has a Mennonite brand name on it, great. If it chooses a different brand name, okay. We learn something from each of those.

Rick: Is that more Jeff Wright speaking, or the attitude of the conference or larger denomination?

Jeff: Mennonite USA is the denomination. We are one of 21 area conferences. I'd like to think that pretty much everyone in the conference would say yes to what I'm advocating, but I'm a realist enough to know that not everybody says it as graciously and generously as I might say it. There are folk for whom it is really important to see our brand name expand. I want that too, but what I really want is for the kingdom to come and for God's will to be done.

Rick: How do you go about connecting with the people you partner with in what you call the "emerging ministries and congregations"?

Jeff: It's a variety of ways that we bump into each other. The one thing that we are committed to in terms of strategy is that we never try to fit a person into a project. We don't start with the project. I can tell you about the next five emerging church leaders and church planters, but I can't tell you about the next five projects. Then we are simply doing the bean counting—how many projects are you getting started. I couldn't care less about the number of projects that get started. We equip leaders—we don't equip projects. And that's a very deliberate choice of language. We don't even really plant churches—we equip church planters. They plant churches. We always begin with the person rather than the project. If a person moves on and the project doesn't have a leader to step in, we pull the plug. If they haven't grown their own leadership to succeed a person, we're not going to parachute somebody in—that's just a recipe for disaster. It's worse than failure. Failure I can live with. It's disasters that I hate.

Rick: You hear some denominations talk about setting goals of planting a certain number of churches within a specific time frame. But it sounds like you don't look at it that way. It sounds to me that you are looking for divine appointments with people who you can work with, you can mentor, you can coach and train, and then let God take it from there.

Jeff: Yes. It really is about seeing where God's doing something and trying to get in line with that. And then letting God use our unique constellation of skills and gifts and abilities in this conference to equip leaders who empower others to line up with God's mission.

Rick: When thinking about Jason and his wife and the ministry they are involved in, what is the biggest thing that excites you and gives you hope?

Jeff: There are two words that come to mind—holistic and organic. Jason is passionate about evangelism. It's just incredible to hear the passion for sharing the good news with people. He's also got a passion for social justice, which is simply another way to share good news with people. The whole evangelism/social action dichotomy that is still a part of my generation is just absent. For there to be a division strikes Jason as weird. That's just so exciting to see. The living out of a holistic gospel as a way of living out good news, as evangelism in action is just powerful to watch. The other piece of it is organic. It's not program-driven—we've to create a preaching point, then put up a building, then we've got to have programs, then get a bigger building, and so on. It's on this organic level of asking how we connect with people. And if we are not the place they connect, that's great. God has another place for them. We trust in the sovereignty of the Holy Spirit to build the church, not in our capacity to grow organizations. Those two adjectives—holistic and organic—are the first things I think of when I think of Jason's ministry.

Rick: What are the biggest challenges that you see for them, but where you might be able to assist them to overcome?

Jeff: The biggest challenge Jason faces in terms of getting traction in ministry is with the financing mechanism for ministry. There are days when I fantasize winning the lottery so I can set up a foundation where I can support people like him in ministry. That hasn't happened and I doubt that it ever will since we don't play the lottery. Not having adequate financial resources to catalyze a project is frustrating for me. What I would wish for Jason and Brooke in their ministry is a clear trajectory into ministry that he has capacity for in terms of his time and availability. Every pastor I work with in Southern California [about 80 credentialed people in their conference], all of them are bi-vocational. We have pastors who give full-time, but are not salaried on our denominational scale full- time. I would wish for Jason a group of comrades, a cohort group of leaders who really live that vision in San Diego with him, so together they move forward in ministry.

Rick: What can you do in your position, or as a conference of churches, to make things like this happen?

Jeff: There are seven things we can do. The first thing is *intercession*. If we aren't praying about it, nothing is going to happen anyway. You've got to start there. There's got to be a strong intercessory foundation to make anything happen. Secondly, we can *train*. That's what the whole school for urban mission project that Jason is a part of is about. Training pastors with a common worldview and a common grammar about ministry in southern California is really important. Third, we can *consult*—in terms of trouble-shooting, helping to build capacity, doing some of the heavy lifting around research projects where one doesn't have all the tools to move from point A to point B. *Coaching* is the fourth one—being engaged in relationships of encouragement. We are saying yes you may, yes you can, yes you will—giving a lot of permission. I find a lot of young people are afraid of people in my position because they've come to perceive them as permission withholders. I'm a huge believer in forgiveness and I believe in the power of failure as a learning environment. I want to see Jason Evans-sized holes in the wall all the time because he's run through the wall somewhere full speed ahead. The fifth one is *connecting* our local churches with the work of the denomination and with the greater cause of the kingdom of God. Number six is *credentialing*—putting the right piece of paper in their hand and saying they have official sanction, making sure people know that they are supported and can move forward in ministry. And the seventh is to *create* avenues for people to gather for worship and celebration, for "explosions of joy." Out of that, new life and energy are created.[6]

---

6. Jeff had the pleasure of hearing Lesslie Newbigin (who was 90 years old and

Rick: If you were to address a gathering of denominational church leaders and alternative church planters like Jason, what would you say?

Jeff: Identity and mission are two sides to the same coin. That coin is the kingdom, or the reign of God. Without identity, mission dissolves very quickly into marketing strategies and technologies. It's important for churches to be distinctive. It's important for Presbyterians to be Presbyterians, for Vineyard to be Vineyard, and it's important for Mennonites to be Mennonites. No one denomination has all the truth—no one expression of Christianity captures all of God's imagination. I think that's why we have denominations in this world. I'm not somebody who thinks denominations are sinful or the result of our brokenness or lack of unity. I think we have this infinite God, and none of us can get all of our minds around him, so we can't know all of God. So, denominations become a way for us to capture what we can capture. We need to respect each other and celebrate who we are. So, identity is important. Without identity, we become marketers and we become engineers and sloganeers, rather than evangelists with good news.

Rick: Any other thoughts you might share at such a gathering?

Jeff: Traditionalists, in our Mennonite context, are really big on identity. One of the questions I always get asked is, "What was Mennonite about that group of people?" So mission without identity is marketing. But the converse has to be highlighted—identity without mission simply becomes celebrations of the past, ethnic pep rallies, and cloistered ghettoized gatherings of people wearing way too much Jesus junk. Identity and mission challenge each other, sharpen each other, correct each other, and hopefully inspire each other. I like to tell the story of Jason picking up a second hand copy of John Howard Yoder's book, *The Politics of Jesus*, and reading it over a weekend and how that transformed his life. When I tell that story to people in the Mennonite church, their mouths drop open. "You mean somebody from outside read John Howard Yoder and liked it and identifies with historic, Anabaptist values?" Yes, why wouldn't that happen? Most Mennonites are so apologetic about their history and tradition that their identity becomes a boundary,

---

nearly blind at the time) speak at a conference, where he said, "All mission begins with an explosion of joy."

a barrier, rather than an invitation. Identity and mission that are invitational are always about drawing people into the presence of God. And so that's what I would say to those two groups: You need each other and can learn from each other.

AUTHOR'S REFLECTION

A Piece of the Darkness

I was blown away when Jason made the comment about being called to respond when he and his fellow brothers and sisters in arms see darkness at work in the city. He said they wanted "a piece of it" . . . a piece of the darkness. It's their call to action . . . reminding me of the expression, "a piece of the action." As individual followers of Christ and as members of local churches, what is your call to action? From where you live, can you see a specific piece of the darkness that threatens individuals and families in your local community? If so, can you identify the action needed in order to confront it? Just imagine if all of us went after a piece of it—a piece of the action—a piece of the darkness. Just how far reaching might our impact be in our neighborhoods, towns, and cities? But in order to get a piece of the action, it will require a trip across the street to see and understand the darkness at work in your city. This calls for people who are willing to go. Find those people and do all you can to help them in their crossing.

Darkness cannot be overcome and displaced by light until light enters into darkened areas. So that's why we need to be there—simply there—in the darkness. You might think you can stand on one side of the street and direct the beam of a high-powered flashlight into the darkness on the other side. But that's ineffective. For one thing, darkness hides around corners and can only be exposed up close, by venturing around those corners with light in hand and heart. Furthermore, confronting darkness is not easy. It's not as simple as identifying what's wrong with the world and broadcasting that they all have to come over to your side of the street and get fixed. Few will hear the broadcast, and even fewer will listen. Even more telling is that this approach is impersonal, void of relationship and human contact. Then why do we tend to prefer this approach? Because it's easy. The more difficult way requires following The

Way—a way that leads to face-to-face, eyeball-to-eyeball relationships with people who might make us uncomfortable.

But it only makes sense that the way of Jesus inevitably leads to making connections, for the root of darkness usually starts from a breakdown in relationship. Therefore, it takes close proximity of Christ's ministers with those in broken relationships to bring about restoration. It takes those who are seeking wholeness, and those who are being healed and restored of broken relationships with God and people, to bring that light across the street and demonstrate its illuminating and healing power. It takes the touch of a street crosser in the name of Jesus. It's a divine and human touch all in one, and we simply can't touch people in this way by staying on our side of the street.

Yet when we use the term "darkness" to denote an absence of light and a propensity toward evil, or to refer to those on the other side of the street as those "living in darkness," we must be extremely careful. We must guard our hearts and minds against allowing such conceptual imagery to skew our perspective of and attitude toward normal people. They are not the enemy. They are not "evil." Their struggles with the issues of life, their desire to find meaning and authenticity in living is no less real than that of the most pious and devout Christians. They are created in the image of God to the same degree as the most revered saints throughout church history. Normal people (those on the other side of the street) are precious people, invaluable people, and priceless people.

So riding into this discussion on our religious high horses is not justified. We should not automatically identify ourselves with "light." Yes, we claim to know the One who is light, and claim that we reflect that light; some of us brightly, but some of us not so much, and others of us, perhaps, not at all. So we must never lose sight of the fact that there is also darkness in the church. One way it is manifested is in our inability to see our shortcomings or even to admit that darkness exists within ourselves. We sometimes choose to linger in the shadows of our own imaginations of what we think it means to be holy, creating delineations between the "good guys" and the "bad guys," between "us" and "them." Another way darkness is manifested in the church is when we refuse to admit that we don't have all the answers to what it really means to be the church. We protect our church traditions, structures, and systematic theologies with unyielding devotion, often to the point of becoming arrogant and condescending toward those Jesus bled and died for. Religious darkness is as real, divisive, and debilitating as any other form of darkness that covers the face of the earth. This sobering reality should always serve to quicken humility in our lives, and move us to see those on the other side of the street with divine compassion, and with profound respect and awe. "Red and yellow, black and white, they are precious in his sight."[7]

The Least, the Last, and the Lost

During my first interview with Jason, he repeatedly used an expression that I believe can be used as a telling indicator of the kind of ministry we value and emphasize: "the least, the last, and the lost." Make an honest ministry appraisal of the church to which you belong by evaluating how you spend your time, energy, and resources. Once your church members are fed, ministered to, and cared for, how many baskets are left over to feed the world? I don't think it's too farfetched to think that the number of baskets we have left over to share with those across the street is an accurate measure of the priorities we hold collectively in our local churches and faith communities—perhaps not the only measure, but a significant one, nonetheless.

How do you measure up? I don't mean in the sense of comparing yourself with the Jones's church on the street corner across from yours. But how do you measure up in terms of the values of the kingdom? How do you measure up to the ways of Jesus? Beyond leftover basket counting, if we are going to look at a baseline measurement for a place to begin our discussion about priorities of the kingdom and seizing our piece of the darkness, what better place to begin our search than to look at the life of Jesus?

Jesus Was a Missionary

How did Jesus live his life? How did he spend his time? An honest examination of the gospels with these questions in mind reveals what I believe Jesus profoundly knew as his core purpose, and what he wholeheartedly embraced as his role in order to fulfill that purpose. Jesus had a mission, so Jesus became a missionary—and a street-crossing one at that. It is a core purpose and role that we should consider as well.

7. Clare Herbert Woolston, "Jesus Loves the Little Children."

There is a well-known passage taken from the Gospel of Luke that is frequently cited with regard to the nature of Jesus' ministry. Eugene Peterson's rendering of this passage is right to the point: "God's Spirit is on me; he's chosen me to preach the Message of good news to the poor, sent me to announce pardon to prisoners and recovery of sight to the blind, to set the burdened and battered free, to announce, 'This is God's year to act!'"[8] Wow! God wants a piece of the action—a piece of the darkness! And Jesus answered this call to action and set into motion the course for those who would join this mission and exemplified the lifestyle for those who would follow after him.

Most scholars believe Jesus was essentially quoting from Isaiah 61. But there is a lesser known passage in Isaiah that parallels this charge and draws particular attention to darkness and light: "I have set you among my people to bind them to me, and provided you as a lighthouse to the nations, to make a start at bringing people into the open, into light: opening blind eyes, releasing prisoners from dungeons, emptying the dark prisons."[9] Bringing light to dark dungeons and releasing those who are imprisoned in them is a major part of the mission. And it requires missionaries—street crossers—to enter those dungeons wherever they may be. And that's exactly where Jesus went and spent most of his time.

Jesus was a true missionary. He was the prime example of what it means to be a street crosser. As I read from the beginning of Matthew through the end of John's Gospel, it's overwhelming to me that the focus of Jesus' ministry was to the poor, the sick, the down-trodden, the down-and-outers, the outcasts, the ostracized, the unclean, the societal rejects, and even the party crowd. So much so that Jesus developed a reputation of being a drunkard and a winebibber. Why? Was it because he was frequently intoxicated? No. It was because he was frequently *with* *those* who were intoxicated, those considered unclean and rejected by society. It was guilt by association. "The Son of Man came eating and

---

8. Luke 4:18–19 (The Message). A more familiar translation of this text from the New International Version reads, "The Spirit of the Lord is on me, because he has anointed me to preach the good news to the poor. He has sent me to proclaim freedom to the prisoners and recovery of sight to the blind, to release the oppressed, and to proclaim the year of the Lord's favor."

9. Isaiah 42:6–7 (The Message).

drinking, and they say, 'He is a glutton and a drunkard, a friend of tax collectors and sinners.' But wisdom is proved right by her actions."[10]

There is little mention of Jesus "going to church" in the gospel accounts. Yes, he visited the synagogue, and probably quite frequently during his ministry at first. But where it is recorded that he was in a synagogue, he was usually challenging the religious people of the day, particularly the scribes and Pharisees. He also preached to the masses on occasion, so one could argue that he wouldn't be opposed to preaching at modern-day megachurches. But the gospels give us a sense that Jesus' daily routine and standard M.O. consisted of being on the go, walking down and crossing over the dusty roads of Galilee. And one more thing to note here: Jesus took a small company of followers with him as he walked and crossed those dusty streets. Elton Trueblood refers to that small band of Christ followers as "a company of danger."[11] This small band joined Jesus as apprentices in his missionary journey, learning his ways up close and personal, taking notes on what would be required of them as journeymen street crossers and simple church planters in the years ahead. So, in one sense, Jesus was a missionary to a religious culture—the culture of the scribes and Pharisees. But in another sense, he was also a missionary to the culture of the hurting, the outcasts, the rejected, the ostracized, and the unclean.

Neil Cole describes the cost and danger of being a missionary this way: "If you want to win this world to Christ, you are going to have to sit in the smoking section."[12] This really hits the nail on the head. Think about it. It graphically illustrates the cost involved in being a street crosser. I believe this describes an aspect of what Trueblood meant by being called to "a company of danger." It means laying down personal preference and familiar settings by choosing to be in a cultural and social setting that is uncomfortable or even offensive to us. But why subject ourselves to "smoke-filled" environments? We should do so for the sake of others. Don't worry, though. Sitting in the smoking section doesn't necessarily mean you will take up smoking, or any other activity that you

10. Matthew 11:19 (NIV).

11. Trueblood writes, "If we realize that Christ was organizing a genuine 'company' many points become clear. Herein is the significance of the cryptic 'Follow me.' He was not advising people to go to church, or even to attend the synagogue; He was, instead, asking for recruits in a company of danger. He was asking not primarily for belief, but for commitment with consequent involvement." *The Company of the Committed*, 34.

12. Cole, *Organic Church*, xxvii.

might find offensive, improper, indecent, or outrageous. Jesus has your back covered—covered by his grace—covered by a strength of compassion that moved him to sit in smoking sections all over the Galilean countryside. As he crisscrossed its dusty roads in search of those in need of a physician, a counselor, a liberator, and a friend, he was not inhibited by fear. It was compassion that drove his purpose and mission to the darkest corners of Galilee.

The question we should really ask ourselves that cuts to the crux of the matter has to do with our purpose and mission, and it's a question that reveals if we really do have compassion for those across the street: What do we value more—being content and well serviced in our smoke-free church settings, or traveling the highways and byways of everyday life where people work and live? Though these two values are not mutually exclusive—church meetings and missional church life—which one typically consumes most of our time, energy, and resources?

For the Love of the Riffraff

I was raised from infancy in church life steeped in the holiness tradition. For those of you unfamiliar with this tradition, it is based on the belief that the Holy Spirit bestows grace to Christ followers so that they can live with power over sin, to those who set their lives apart for the purposes of God. Personal holiness and sanctification are very demanding and powerful theological tenets, and ones that holiness teachers say can be experienced by all devoted and consecrated followers of Jesus. "Wherefore come out from among them, and be ye separate, saith the Lord and touch not the unclean thing; and I will receive you."[13] This Bible verse was a battle cry very familiar to me growing up under the teachings of sanctification-preaching pastors and evangelists. This scriptural call, one that Paul gave to the Corinthians, had a well-intended purpose; to call people into the kingdom of God, into a new way of living life in the midst of a culture governed by narcissism, self-centeredness, and ethnocentric attitudes. This is great teaching, in theory, and sometimes even approachable in practice, but it has often morphed into unintended attitudes and consequences. Growing up, this exhortation to set oneself apart to God and holy living was often pronounced in the following manner: "Don't dance, drink, cuss, or chew, and don't go with girls that

13. 2 Corinthians 6:17 (KJV).

do!" In other words, your body is the temple of God, so don't desecrate it with unholy behavior, and don't even associate with those exhibiting "worldly" behavior! Here's yet another way I interpreted this plea from the pulpits of my youth: "Come out from the unclean, and go be with the righteous—and thus protect yourselves behind the walls of your church buildings."

Wow! This no longer sounds to me like the voice of Jesus, nor is it exemplified by his life that we read about in the gospels! Think about this . . . In the church we claim that Jesus was the holiest man who has ever lived in human history. Yet he chose to spend most of his time hanging out with the "unclean." It appears to me that it wasn't a matter of "coming out from" the surrounding culture in order to protect himself from sin, or a matter of rejecting an unbelieving and perverse people. No way! Consider the story recorded in the second chapter of the Gospel of Mark where Jesus is hanging out with "disreputable guests." The religious leaders confronted Jesus and said, "What kind of example is this, acting cozy with the riffraff?"[14] What a great question! "What kind of example is this?" Answer: It's an awesome and profound example! It's the example of the most Holy One, the greatest example of what it means to be set apart for the purposes of God.

Don't be afraid of the dark. Don't be afraid to get your hands dirty. Don't be afraid to sit in the smoking section for the sake of others! We love to speak boldly of our forgiveness in Christ who has cleansed us from the guilt of our sin, and boldly and joyfully we should. But can we speak boldly and joyfully about another type of guilt—one that we should *not* cleanse from ourselves—a guilt by association? For our Lord was strongly accused of this—guilt by association with the unclean, those of disrepute—the riffraff! This was the reputation he earned from the most devout churchgoers of his day, and if I might say so, a reputation that he proudly received as one who came to minister to those on the other side of the street.

I have a good friend I first met in college. We used to call him "Burnside Kurt."[15] He got that name from the reputation he earned by the amount of time he spent walking the street of Burnside—the "skid row" part of downtown Portland, Oregon. Kurt was, and still is today,

---

14. Mark 2:13–17 (The Message).

15. Kurt Salierno has authored four books. To learn about his books and ministry on the street, visit http://www.kurtsalierno.com.

a literal street crosser. It's what he calls having "church on the street." He has given his life to the "riffraff" of our society more than anyone I personally know. On any given day, you might find Kurt sleeping in an alley cuddled up for warmth next to a homeless man, or living under a freeway overpass or in the bushes for a few days in a "bum city." Kurt isn't afraid of sitting in the smoking section, or putting his life on the line by being in the company of danger. On more than one occasion, Kurt has been threatened by gangs, shot at, and stabbed. In explaining to others why he chooses to minister under such dark conditions to the homeless, drug addicts, and prostitutes, I've heard Kurt say that it brings him great joy to know that he is ministering to and loving his Lord when he does so "to one of the least of these."[16] When it comes to being a follower in the ways of Jesus, what brings you great joy?

How to Change the World with a Light Bulb

Maybe hearing an inspirational sermon brings you great joy. I must admit that I enjoy hearing a good sermon, now and then. Inspiration is powerful, and so are words. But how many sermons does it take to change the world? It seems we spend an inordinate amount of time clustered together around pulpits hoping to hear something that will change our lives and make us better Christians. How many hours a week do we need to hear what is essentially the same message, spoken and presented in a myriad of ways, intended to inspire us to go change the world? Maybe it's time for me to go more, come less; serve more, listen less; love others more, myself less. Maybe it's time for a little less coming to listen for our own sakes, and time for a little more going to serve for the sake of others.

How many sermons does it take to change the world? Unlike the answer to a familiar riddle involving light bulbs, it doesn't take a multitude of inept individuals to bring about a change. It only takes one sermon, and that sermon is you. And the world that needs changing is just across the street. So cross the street and change it.

When you cross, always remember that you are a signpost pointing the way to Jesus. The apostle Paul put it this way: "You show that you are a letter from Christ, written not with ink but with the Spirit of the living God, not on tablets of stone but on tablets of human hearts."[17] Think about

16. Matthew 25:40 (NKJV).
17. 2 Corinthians 3:3 (NIV).

it! We are the living letters of Christ—animated Bibles with legs—legs that can carry us across the street, bringing colorful detail to the gospel and hope to those in darkness. Jesus echoes this idea: "Let your light shine before men in such a way that they may see your good works, and glorify your Father who is in heaven."[18] We are like divinely inspired or "aspirated" light bulbs. Just as many incandescent light bulbs are filled with inert gas for the purpose of increasing output and longevity, we too are filled with the very breath of God—aspirated by his life—that we might radiate with divine light and illuminate darkened lives. It only takes one little light bulb to illuminate a darkened room, or a darkened heart.

Going Public

Jesus said, "Let me tell you why you are here. You're here to be light, bringing out the God-colors in the world. God is not a secret to be kept. We're going public with this, as public as a city on a hill. If I make you light-bearers, you don't think I'm going to hide you under a bucket, do you?"[19] This gives new meaning to the term "going public" for church planting. It's more than a strategic point in time when we inform the community that a new church exists by hanging flyers on doorknobs and implementing mass mailings. Going public is a real spectacle, but not in the usual church planting sense—not in the sense of a "come-to-us in order to see a showy exhibition." Rather, going public means going *to* the public, in order to reveal the hope and light of Christ to those not willing to come to us. Think of it this way: *we are* the spectacle—a changed people who live life with meaning for the sake of others. Furthermore, we are *spectacles*—the lenses through which the public can see Jesus up close and personal, no longer hidden behind four walls, or under a bucket.

When it comes to the church and our consumer mindset toward receiving spiritual services, maybe it's time to return to our intended identity as a people who follow after the example of Jesus—people of hope and light. Instead of using vast amounts of our resources and energy to change one person—one light bulb—think of it in terms of one light changing the world. And then think about the potential of what a group of lights together can accomplish in piercing the darkness! As powerful as our individual testimonies might be, there is something that carries an even

18. Matthew 5:16 (NASB).
19. Matthew 5:13–15 (The Message).

greater light: our corporate testimony as we live life together as followers of Jesus. So cross the street together. Demonstrate his life—together—in foreign mission fields that are as close as the homes behind the fences in your backyards. Remember that, as followers of Jesus, we were never instructed by our Lord to hide from outsiders by circling our wagons together in order to withstand assaults from the darkness. No. But an example has been shown us and instructions given to leave our wagons behind that we might go and get a piece of the action—a piece of the darkness—by crossing over into the darkness with the *peace* of the Light.

FOR PERSONAL REFLECTION AND GROUP DISCUSSION

1. Jason used the phrase, "the least, the last, and the lost." Who are these people in your life, in your neighborhood, and in your town or city? How does your local church go out of its way to make a place for them, to reach out to them in a significant way?

2. Have you or your church body, in essence, earned a reputation of being a "drunkard" through guilt by association? What does that mean in your specific situation? What label have you earned? If you have yet to earn a reputation, with what cause or people group do you desire to associate?

3. Identify your "piece of the action," your piece of the darkness (personally and/or as a community of faith). Think about or discuss what it would require for your local church to partner with a simple church planter as a way to get a piece of the action.

4. If you are a simple church planter or a member of a small faith community, what stands in your way of entering dark places with the light of the gospel?

5. Do you agree with the observation that many churches spend a disproportionate amount of time and resources on "serving the saints" in Sunday morning worship events? If so, does that include your local church? What visible indicators reveal or reflect your ministry priorities as a local church body?

6. Reflect on the positive attributes of your local worship service gatherings, and then discuss how these attributes contribute to furthering a missional presence of your church body in your town or city.

3

Simply Together

HOME IS WHERE THE CHURCH IS

"I WAS BORN ON the front pew, as they say," remarks Jess Hutchison, a simple church planter in Portland, Oregon. "I'm old school, fourth generation. I don't know if that's a good thing or a bad thing, but I am." His family goes back four generations in the Church of God—Anderson, Indiana, variety. Jess reflects,

> I was a typical church kid in a lot of ways because I grew up in church with grandparents and great grandparents, all attending the same church when I was growing up. So I had a lot of that foundational spiritual guidance and heritage. While that doesn't amount to eternity, it does set a pretty nice table for a young guy like me growing up in that environment and having the support of my family around me. I always like to tell people that I've had every opportunity to succeed, and if I screwed up, it was my own fault.

Jess's story is similar to that of many of us who grew up in the church. As a church kid he did all the "churchy things," as he puts it, referring to the usual activities church kids experience, and later being part of all the action a youth group provides for teenagers. His wife, Laura, had similar experiences while growing up as a "PK" (pastor's kid) in the home of a Church of God pastor. As high school sweethearts, Jess and Laura were part of the same youth group.

> We didn't go to the same high school, but we spent all kinds of time together at church. Our families knew each other really well. And my parents were involved in leadership and [Laura's] dad was the pastor of the church. It was a fishbowl for a lot of

the time we were dating as kids. If we didn't sit together during a service, then people would start talking and chitchatting about it. All that stuff was very foundational in what I really value about church, and what I don't like about it as well.

Besides his high school sweetheart, Jess had another love: he loved to play football. He played the game at a high level, excelling in the sport to such a degree that he made the varsity team as a sophomore in high school. But at the height of becoming a talented football player, Jess sensed that his devotion to the game was infringing upon his devotion to God, and that God was asking him to give it up entirely. Jess recalls,

> As part of my own story, basically I made this choice between my sophomore and junior years to stop playing football. That was really hard on me because I really felt lost, and I felt that God didn't replace it with anything. He just made it obvious that I needed to give it up. My junior year, I was really wandering, not spiritually necessarily, but almost in a frustrated, angry kind of way at God, because I really felt like he took away the one thing I cared about.

But apparently, God had something else in mind. The year he gave up football was the same year he started dating Laura. In addition, it was the summer between his junior and senior years of high school that Jess felt called to ministry. He was at a church camp when he sensed a strong leading to ministry during a worship service. Jess remembers,

> I felt this overwhelming sense. It wasn't like lightning bolts and audible voices, or anything like that, but this overwhelming sense of "This is what I'm replacing [football] with—the passion for people." I just began sobbing uncontrollably. Nothing had ever happened to me like that before. But it was very vivid and very real. Laura, my girlfriend at the time, came up to me after the service and asked me, "Are you going to do it?" And I was like, "What?" And she said, "Are you going to be a pastor?" And I almost felt like saying, "Are you kidding?" Laura said, "Yes, I just felt like I was supposed to ask you this question." It was confirming in a lot of ways, but specifically confirming that very night. I couldn't turn my back on that because it was too real. It might as well have been a lightning bolt in my mind and heart.

From that point on, Jess set his sights on church life and ministry. After graduation from high school in 1995, he enrolled at Warner Pacific College—a Church of God-affiliated college in Portland, Oregon, just north of his hometown of Albany. While majoring in religion and Christian ministries, he became heavily involved working with youth groups in the Portland area. But during his sophomore year at Warner, Jess began a search for answers to questions that were surfacing in his mind.

> I wasn't questioning my faith, but church. I just remembered thinking that many of the churches I had been to just had a lot of people who all agreed to go there and lie to each other every week. For example, "How are you this week?" And people would say, "We're doing great." And everybody knew they really weren't okay. And yet, that's as deep as the questions went, and that's as deep as the questions [were intended] to go. Week in and week out, people weren't honest with themselves or honest with the people around them. They felt some sort of pressing obligation to go and continue to do that. It just seemed so odd to me. I knew that it didn't have to be like that, and that wasn't the church that Christ wanted. I had in the back of my mind this thought: "I can't do it the normal way."

During his junior year in college, Jess served as a part-time youth pastor for a church that met on the college campus. It was somewhat different than your typical church. It was led by one of his professors and attended by a lot of different thinkers—a collection of college professors and disgruntled folks from other churches. Jess didn't know their personal histories or why they attended this particular gathering. But when he arrived on the scene, he sensed that many of them were wounded and in need of healing. "They were all there for a specific reason. A lot of it was church, but a lot of it was for healing, too." His position with this church continued through the rest of his college days at Warner.

Jess's next ministry experience came after he and Laura were married in 1998. From 1999 to 2004, Jess held a position with Youth For Christ while at the same time he worked as a youth pastor for the Church of God in Rainier, Oregon. This dual role was to his liking. "The reason I did that was I didn't want to do a traditional youth pastor gig, where I was made to do a bunch of office hours and do a lot of things I didn't want to do." Jess wanted the freedom to go to high school campuses as much as possible, go to high school sporting events, and visit in the homes and hangouts of high school students. He wanted this relational kind of youth ministry rather than being consumed with typical Wednesday night youth meetings, Sunday morning routines, along with all the other monthly activities and periodic youth retreats. Jess remembers, "I didn't want that to be the focus. I wanted relationships to be the focus. I didn't want to abandon [church functions]. I still intended to go and participate and do all that stuff." But the idea of sitting behind a desk was something Jess found troubling. "I didn't see the value in it and I really resisted that idea," he recalls. He thought there had to be a way to do ministry that wasn't necessarily traditional, but afforded him the chance to create his own niche. He was able to develop this style at the church in Rainier.

> I got the infrastructure in place and the idea that [the church] wouldn't necessarily see me in the office all the time. But I had some [struggles] over that with some people in the church who thought I should probably do it a different way, because their idea of a youth pastor was to fit a traditional model, [and] I was not doing that. They wanted more big events where we give the salvation message, but I wanted to hang out with their sons and daughters and with their friends. I wanted to embody salvation rather than tell them about it.

Jess wanted to minister to youth in a way that made them feel like they were part of the church, even before they realized it, something more organic and natural. It was an approach to youth ministry that appeared, by some in the congregation, to be at odds with more familiar methods that sought to increase attendance at youth events. Jess recalls, "I kept saying, 'That's not the point.' But for folks who have been in church all their lives, that is the point. I think I drove them nuts." Upon reflection, Jess looks back now with more understanding and sympathy for the other point of view. "I was probably rude about it when I shouldn't have been."

In 2004, Jess left his position in Rainier on good terms with great relationships intact. With a quiver full of ministry tools and skills he had acquired as a youth pastor, he was ready to move on from a traditional ministry context. Even though he hadn't functioned as a typical youth pastor, he did get a taste for more traditional duties. For instance, when the senior pastor resigned from the church in Rainier, Jess had to pick up the slack and step into the normal pastoral roles of visitations, funerals, and preaching. It was a time for personal growth and new experiences, but it did not change his idealism; it only served to enforce his convictions. Jess recalls, "In a time of the greatest need when we didn't have a pastor, the church wasn't able to care for itself. We were so dependent on that one guy to come and be and do for everybody in the whole entire church and be there for them." Being thrust into an interim role as lead pastor brought with it a vantage point from which Jess would see and experience realities in the ministry that only confirmed his longing to find a more effective, holistic, and personally satisfying way to serve the church.

> I specifically remember going to somebody's bedside when they were sick in the hospital. I prayed with them. I remember getting a comment afterwards, "It's too bad we don't have a pastor to come and be with us." I just had this sick feeling—not that it was a punch in my gut, but that they didn't see one another. There were people all over the room—family members and church members. There were people everywhere caring for them, but they had this mentality that some sort of heroic pastor figure had to do that for them. It really broke my heart.

This experience caused Jess to think more deeply about fundamental questions concerning how ministry is performed in the church. Jess thought to himself, "What if we could all look at each other and be the priesthood of all believers, and we could care for one another's needs, and it didn't have to be one specific person that did all these things for you?" Jess desired for others in the church to understand and embrace mutual responsibility for one another. He wanted them to realize that when a brother or sister in Christ visited someone in the hospital, a pastor was essentially ministering to that person.

Jess recalls situations when the church didn't have enough money to help people in the community. He found himself in church business meetings, going over line items in the budget while the congregation felt unable to help with specific physical needs, even for their own people in the church. They needed to be cared for, even monetarily, Jess thought.

> I'm sitting there thinking, "But we do have the money. We're just spending it in other ways." And that got me thinking about, alongside this priesthood of all believers thing, what if I didn't have to be paid by the church? Then that money could go do something else for somebody else.

Jess believed this kind of shift would move people to be more dependent on one another, and not solely on an employee to do the job. Otherwise, congregants begin to expect the vocational pastor to visit the sick and "do" the work of the ministry. "It's a part of their job description," Jess comments. "But if you weren't paying somebody to do it, then it just makes sense that everybody should pitch in and help."

SOMETIMES A WINDING ROADS LEADS HOME

Experiences like these helped to lead Jess down a new road. They served to form a philosophy of church life and ministry for Jess and Laura, shaping their thinking about church planting several years prior to leaving the church in Rainier. But before leaving his post in Rainier, Jess met up with Marcus Dorsey, a fellow youth pastor in the Church of God. They were at a youth pastor's retreat, and the two of them stayed up into all hours of the night talking about church, about what it might look like.

> We just found this kindred spirit immediately, and realized that there's more than just us out there. I had felt really isolated in a lot of ways because my peers weren't of the same mindset. If you go tell a senior pastor that you don't want to get paid, then that's kind of like a direct assault on their vocation. They think you're trying to be critical, but that's not what I was trying to do. I just wanted to try to do things in a different way.

Jess and Marcus talked of a day down the road when they might plant a church together. Jess recalls thinking, "If God would point us in that direction, we would love to do church together, to be church together." Their idea wasn't so much that they would go and "do church" as it was for them to "be church together." Jess says, "It wasn't a location as much as a presence. We wanted to embody the body of Christ together. We decided if God opened those doors, then we could [do it]. If not, then we'd still have each other to talk theology and church with, at least commiserate with."

The year leading up to Jess's new friendship with Marcus, he and Laura were trying to start a family, but without success. "It was a terribly dark time in my life. I was making all these important decisions during this time of misery in our lives when we couldn't have kids. I felt like God was mad at us. I knew theologically that wasn't the case, but it sure felt like it." But in March of 2005, his theology was proven right—with their first son, Isaac. The twins followed two years later, Minnie and Ezekiel—further evidence that God wasn't mad.

After his resignation from the youth pastor position in Rainier, Jess found employment in the admissions department at Warner Pacific College. It afforded Jess and Laura the chance to return to Portland and the opportunity to plant a different kind of church with his friend, Marcus. After much prayer, they decided to make the move. One of Jess's questions of concern was if the new job would actually interfere with planting and pastoring a church. It was the first time they actually stepped out from a traditional ministry setting to embrace something very unknown to them; it would be the first time Jess would find employment outside of the church to put food on the table, as well as the first attempt at church planting.

> I say church plant, but it really wasn't in that sense. I didn't intend to go and canvas the neighborhoods and get a core group of people, attend trainings. I just wanted to simply, like you said, Rick, do "simple church." I wanted to see if there were other people who had a like-minded, kindred spirit with us and see what would happen.

Because of their close ties and family connections within the Church of God, it wasn't as simple as slipping away into obscurity to start a new kind of church. When they resigned from the church in Rainier in order to plant a church in Portland, people heard about it right away through their network of friends and associates.

> When we resigned from Rainier and said we're going to move to Portland and start a church, their first comment to us was, "Okay, where do you need the money and how fast can we get it to you?" But that's not what we wanted and that's not what we were doing. So it was sort of weird for them because they really didn't know what to do with us, and we really didn't know what to do with them. I'm an ordained Church of God pastor, so I have some responsibility to keep them up-to-date on what I'm doing and why I'm doing it. I felt like I needed to do that. It wasn't like I was trying to be secretive about it. They were offering all these different trainings on how to start churches, and I really resisted that stuff, especially since I was going to Portland to take a job. I didn't have time, and I didn't want to do them, anyway. But it eventually came down to them requesting that we be officially a part of the Church of God, and how can this be like a real congregation, for a lack of a better way to say it.

Jess and Marcus didn't start the church for about one year. "Both of us were really, really Church of God. We didn't just get up and start a church without seeing a lot of other models out there." In the meantime, Marcus kept his youth pastor position. It was up to Jess to do some of the initial legwork. From October of 2004 through the summer of 2005, Jess went to a different church almost every weekend. He recalls attending churches of various traditions—old, new, high church, Pentecostal, and church plants.

I just wanted to see what was out there. The best part of that whole thing was that I pretty much scrapped what I had seen that whole year, because it wasn't about a model, it wasn't about a program. It was simply about being with each other and celebrating the life of Christ. And that can be done in a lot of different ways, and it didn't have to be done in any particular way.

During this time of exploration, research, and soul-searching as to the kind of church they should plant, Jess emailed a good friend explaining to him the difficult process he was going through in trying to determine how to go start and what it should look like. "What good parts of each church do I use and what bad parts of each do I throw out?" Jess remembers writing. His friend replied back to Jess with a very simple but sobering question, "Who are you to decide what part you keep and what part you throw out?"

He basically said that we stand in a stream of 2,000 years of church history, and that's a pretty important chunk of your history and development. I'm not smart enough and you're not smart enough to go picking and choosing the parts of the church you like and don't like. There's a lot to be said for tradition and things that have been around for ages without changing. He basically told me to be very careful in trying to pick and choose what you think church might look like. It was very convicting for me.

Jess was stunned. It was as if his heart was laid wide open for the world to see. His friend's words went deep, causing Jess to look back and evaluate his true motives for wanting to do church differently. "I was kind of on this high horse, this pedestal of 'I'm going to do church the right way,'" Jess recalls. It was as though his friend had challenged Jess to go back to his church, apologize for his arrogance, and simply sit there, be quiet, and just be a part of the church. "Oh gosh, he's so right," Jess thought. "That would have been the most Christian thing I could do." He began to realize that many church planters before him were guilty of the same attitude, the same kind of pick-and-choose your favorite preferences for church life. Jess remembers,

At that time, the emerging church was into using candles. [They said], "We're going to read some of the old things of the church, and we're going to reclaim some of the old things that were important to the church back then." But really, what they were doing was picking and choosing what they thought would be most meaningful, when that's not necessarily the right thing to do.

DON'T STRAY TOO FAR FROM HOME

This email from Jess's friend was a very sobering eye-opener. It laid Jess's heart wide open, and Marcus's, too. Subsequently, this led to their first decision as to how to go about planting a church: they wanted to remain with the Church of God. Jess remembers, "Even though we saw a lot of flaws with the Church of God and [had] a lot of frustrations with the Church of God, it was who we were and are and continue to be—it's a part of our story," says Jess. "It was good for us to submit, whether we liked it or not. That changed us," he adds. Looking back, Jess says it took a lot of the sting away from the conversations they had with pastors around the state of Oregon about what he and Marcus were trying to do. "It wasn't that we were doing something better than they were, it was just that we were doing something different and that we are still a part of them and we would love to have a conversation about this. But not in a way that was oppressive, [as if] we're right and you're wrong."

What would come to be known as the Winding Road Church of God began to gather in the Hutchisons' home in October of 2005— Jess and Laura, Marcus and his wife, Erin, and two college-age girls. A grand total of six adults were "simply together" on a regular basis to discern if committing to one another as a church body was the right thing to do. All signs looked like a green light.

> We are officially in the Church of God yearbook as "Winding Road Church of God." We didn't do "community church." We didn't do just "Winding Road." And we didn't do whatever seemed the least denominational. We did the whole Winding Road Church of God, because [the name] doesn't matter to us. The name wasn't important—it's not like we have t-shirts or any-thing. We don't even have a sign!

It wasn't a financial hurdle they had to jump—not in terms of rent-ing a building or paying a pastor. "In a lot of ways, it was easier than a traditional church plant model. We didn't have a lot of the same worries that other churches had," says Jess. Yet there came a time after meeting at the Hutchison's home that the group started to discuss the idea of having a separate place to meet. It was a difficult corner to negotiate because they didn't want the added expense that comes with a facility. But if it were free, that would be acceptable. And that's exactly what happened— they got access to an older house that had been converted into an office building, free of charge, so long as they cleaned up after their gatherings. It had a large room where they met for worship services.

In their first year, they participated as a group in service projects one Sunday a month—Meals On Wheels through Loaves and Fishes, for example. Jess recalls, "Then [we thought], this is kind of silly, because we are just programming service into peoples' lives. We didn't want institutionalized service." It ended up that Marcus took on Meals on Wheels himself and invited people to go along with him. Instead of programming service, the desire was to see the body reach and serve neighbors and associates in day-to-day living.

> You've got neighbors and friends that need something more than Meals on Wheels. We were up to two or three routes and we had to make sure we had enough people. It felt a lot like church services that we were part of earlier—counting up numbers and how many of this, and can we do more routes. It was unsettling because it was programmed church once again. It was just a different new and improved kind, but it was still the same thing. We were hoping the Meals on Wheels route would be less about the route and more about the people on the route. It was for people doing it every week, like Marcus. He continues to do it because he has relationships with people that he sees on the route. I think that's a great reason to do it, not because you feel obligated.

This early focus on service was a core value for the Winding Road community, but not service at the cost of making it happen through programming. They believed programming service was problematic for more traditional churches and wanted to avoid some of the issues they had observed and experienced in their former faith communities. For example, they thought that people who contributed financially in their former churches were unintentionally made to feel like their ministry was to give money to the church, or that some parishioners misinterpreted the concept of giving. In either case, it gave people the idea that church would do the ministry in their stead. Subsequently, Winding Road wanted to instill a desire to serve in a way that's an outgrowth of one's Christian spirituality. They sought to accomplish this by holding each other accountable for finding ways to serve in one's neighborhood or in the marketplace. Jess reflects on how this value shapes their conversations today:

Now, when we ask people, "How's your week going?"—my ears are definitely listening. Those are great conversations we can have on the side with people about where are you plugging in, how are you serving your neighbors or the people around you. Those are important things for me to listen for as a pastor and continue to teach on those aspects.

WHO SAID DOING CHURCH WAS EASY?

With this core value positioned as a foundational pillar for their young church, a twist in the road occurred when the idea of starting a day care for low-income families surfaced within the group. This time, it wasn't just a matter of whether or not they should use a building rent free, but should they make a commitment, as a church, to purchase a facility to be used as a day care facility? This was a huge decision, not only in terms of the financial cost, but in terms of their philosophy to function as simply and as thriftily as possible. At first glance, buying a facility seemed contradictory to their goals. But the more they prayed about it, the more they sensed God's leading to start a day care for low-income families. So the decision was made to move forward. This small church family purchased a house to be used as a day care facility. Marcus's family owned the house, and made it possible to purchase the home with no down payment. Besides the plan to use it for a day care facility, it was also a place Winding Road could meet as a church. "But it would have been fine to have church anywhere, in my opinion," says Jess. In addition, they acquired free day care supplies from a church that had closed down its day care. The doors for this new venture seemed open, but for one huge obstacle—they couldn't get any kids to come!

"It was so frustrating," recalls Jess. They needed just ten kids to make it self-sustaining without any overhead. "It was great, in theory. But it was a very frustrating [and difficult] moment in the history of our young little church."

With the summer of 2008 approaching, they had to decide what to do with the house and mortgage. Several new families had joined the group around the time the church was trying to make this decision. Obviously, the new members had no emotional attachment to the building. "So, it was sort of providential that God brought these folks on board. They joined in when we were still meeting at the building, and they started asking why we even had a building," Jess recalls.

It was a perplexing situation. Part of their original mission was to be free from the need for a building in order to do ministry. Yet the whole purpose in buying a house was to start a day care that never really got off the ground. "So we were stuck with this building we didn't want and didn't want to pay for. When the new families started asking, we realized we needed to make a change. Since it didn't work, it didn't work," says Jess. "Obedience is far more important in this whole thing than success." So they made the decision as a group to cut their losses. They lost money in the process because it was during the downturn in the housing market. "But we ended up getting it sold," Jess remarks. It wasn't as though they wanted to be a "church building group," but a group of Christians that could be mobile and fluid. This experience reinforced their core values. Jess reflects, "It didn't change the rules of church for us. We jumped in with both feet, didn't look back, and we got scorched a little, but we would do it again. That's the beauty of it."

Still convinced of a tent-maker approach to ministry, Jess pursued a teaching degree, while Marcus went to chiropractic school and is now near completion. Jess reached his goal and graduated with a teaching degree in December of 2008. He was hired as an elementary school teacher in the fall of 2009.

> We're all working people and we all do our forty hours a week wherever we work. But that doesn't let us off the hook. And in fact, those jobs, those vocations, are our means to a better end, which is serving each other and the world. There is no off duty— we just take church wherever we're at and keep going. I know that there are biblical reasons for vocational pastors, but I also see some biblical evidence for tent-making. That's the route we've chosen.

Winding Road Church of God is once again gathering for worship and mutual support in the Hutchisons' home, back where they first started. Much has been learned in their short life together as a faith community, some of it painfully difficult, and some of it quite good and important, particularly concerning relationships. As all churches do, Winding Road has faced their share of difficulties in the life of their young church. One such example involved a couple in their fellowship facing marital problems. But instead of taking "sides" as a church, and in the process cause one or both parties to leave the group, Winding Roads chose to care for and walk with both individuals without judgment. They extended grace to this couple because of their deep commitment to love one another. Jess remarks:

> Even with our current little church right now, we've set it up to be completely honest and open with each other, and it still hurts every time someone does something stupid. But at least we all know about it. That's the ideal. If we're going to screw up, then we all should know about it, right? That's the only way we can help, love, and support.

Through the highs and lows as a young community of faith, there is one thing they're more convinced of than ever before: church truly is all about being a family. It means supporting each other through all the ups and downs of life. Church is all about following Jesus together, no matter what happens. This is the gospel, and it's good news.

Q & A WITH JESS HUTCHISON

The following question and answer session with Jess Hutchison is intended to further the reader's understanding into his philosophy of ministry, what motivates simple church planters to embark on their journeys, and in Jess's case, why it's important to remain accountable to a larger movement or denomination. Interviews were conducted between November of 2008 and January of 2010. Chronological references in the following interview fall within this time frame. As of June 2011, Jess continues to serve as the pastor of Winding Road Church of God and is employed full-time as an elementary school teacher.

Rick: You seem to make a big deal about family, togetherness, and commitment to one another. Where does that come from?

Jess: I had a really unique situation in terms of proximity with my family, as well as spiritual growth with all my family members involved. And I think looking back on that, it provided really fertile soil for my own spiritual development. As I read Scripture, I read it through that lens, in essence. When you look at the book of Acts, [you see] that these people didn't move very far away from each other. Proximity was a big thing and family was a big thing. Sharing life was a big thing, whether that be with family or very close friends. Family is just a great example of how that can work, and some families are so dysfunctional it can't [work]. But families like mine actually provide a really good model for how it could be. And it also provided a model of what close friendships can be. I often equate my own church family now as my family, because proximity-wise, I'm closer to them than I am with my own family. So I liken my current church family often to what I grew up with, in my own multigenerational foundational church experience. That all kind of plays into what we are doing now.

Rick: Speak to your decision and desire to stay connected with the Church of God.

Jess: One of the most significant pieces to this whole thing is that I don't ever want to *not* be Church of God. Not because I think they have all the right answers, but because that's part of the story God placed me in. I'm settled on that. I'm submitting to that, and I'm okay with that. I'm arrogant to think that I can somehow do church better. But I've always been Church of God. That's where I've grown up. It doesn't necessarily change what we do, but it does change whom we are accountable to. And that's important to us. We don't have to do things the Church of God way, but we definitely need to have accountability to our Church of God brothers and sisters, because they are a part of us and who we are. I've talked with other church planters who have come out of denominations and that's kind of where we were at first. And they just don't get it, and I'm not sure I fully understand the submission aspect of this, but I think it's healthy.

Rick: How has your relationship with the Church of God in Oregon been helpful to you?

Jess: That was kind of frustrating [in the beginning] and a blessing at the same time because the Church of God wanted to know how to help us. We kept telling them there's nothing they can really do other than pray for us. They wanted to send money our way, but that wasn't helpful for us. I remember saying to somebody at one point, "Look, if you gave us money we would probably end up giving it to some homeless people or something." We were just trying to be honest with them. We would have probably made a bunch of peanut butter and jelly sandwiches and tried to find way to give them to homeless people, even $2,000 worth, if that's what they gave us! We didn't take any monetary support from the Church of God because it just didn't fit. Money wasn't the issue. And in fact, we had always talked about what if all of our tithes went to ministry stuff and there was no overhead, no salaries to pay. It was never the point to get a big core group of people and come up with a budget. We were really excited about not having red tape to jump through when we heard about a need—we could just do it, we can just meet the need and go for it. That was exciting and refreshing for those of us who had sat in council meetings all our lives. Back then, when somebody had a request, it had to go through a benevolence committee. Now, when we hear about a need, it's so fun just to write a check.

Rick: When you think about helping people or inviting people to be part of your group, whom do you have in mind? What kind of people?

Jess: I guess in terms of "target audience" it would be whoever it is that you work with, live with, or play with. That would be who it is that God's having you minister to. Sometimes there's crossover there, sometimes there's not. I really feel like in a lot of ways that the church's responsibility—and I guess I need to be careful when I say this—isn't to go out and reach your lost friends. It's essentially your job to do that. And so there's certainly not a focus on making sure we have nonbelievers around us all the time at our worship gathering because there's the expectation that you already have nonbelievers around you all the time that you're ministering to. I don't think it's the pastor's job to save your friends. That's your job, you know, and your family, that's your job. The church is really a place of discipleship and celebration, and all those things that build you up to go out and make disciples, that kind of thing. It's not to say that it's not a point of emphasis [evangelism]. I just don't think it's the church's role to do that sort of thing for you. We've hired that job out for too long. I guess that's kind of a soapbox that I like to stand on.

Rick: I'm assuming that those who are walking with you have a similar understanding?

Jess: Exactly. Yeah. I mean that's part of why I guess they've chosen to be with us. . . . We are not trying to attract as many people as possible. That may not be, in our minds, the best methodology.

Rick: So you're a teacher, and that's great, and that's the kind of place you want to be in. But as far as your calling, do you still see yourself as a pastor in terms of deeper motivation?

Jess: Absolutely. So the direction that we took the church in terms of what we study and for caring for one another, there's got be somebody, I guess, who heads that stuff up and teaches everybody how to do it. In that sense I feel pastoral, but it's not in the same sense of a vocational pastor. It's not something I want to garner a check from or get paid to do. It's not even really a title that I seek, but it's more of a role. I think it's pretty fluid. We've gotten so accustomed to hearing the title that goes along with different things in the church, even down to committee members and leaders and democracy—all those things—it's just not essential to me. I think it all comes down to calling, and it should for everybody. And it's not like we do it perfectly at all, because we don't. But, I really want to emphasize the idea that we are the priesthood of all believers. It doesn't take one person to go care for other people of the church, but it's really that everyone should embody that role of caring for one another, evangelism, and discipleship. We are all accountable to one another, not just to one person. That's kind of really important to me, and so in terms of pastoring, I want everyone to be able to see that everyone in our group is able to contribute something to the body and building one another up. That certainly had to happen with me being in school and starting a new job, all these things I had piled on. And so in order for a group to keep functioning, there have to be other people who can do stuff.

Rick: In our discussions, the word "missional" has not really been a part of your vocabulary, but the concept of calling and serving is very much a part of it. If, as you say, it's our purpose as the body of Christ to come alongside each other to help identify each of our callings and to fulfill those callings, wouldn't you say that's one definition of being missional, in the sense that you're releasing the body to go and do what they've been called to do outside the confines of church gatherings?

Jess: Well, I think people have to discover what that is. So much, I think, in recent church history, has been about your vocation and people saying that's their calling. I don't know that's always the case.

I think your vocation is often a means to an end, which is your calling. People stumble into jobs and then they sort of look back reflectively and say, "God led me here." But they were never called to do it, you know. It's a convenient way to say God led them there. Which, I'm not going to argue with them, but at the same time, I'm not sure how much actually did happen that way. But for me, I think God doesn't even necessarily care what you're doing. I mean, he needs people pumping gas just as well as he needs people working at schools and everywhere. There's some element of truth to what [Henri] Nouwen says about your greatest passion intersecting with the world's greatest need, or something like that, which I totally get. But at the same time, I think we sort of overplay some of that vocational stuff, and instead of really seeking out what our calling is, we just sort of default to where we land. And that becomes our calling. It's convenient for folks to just say [that they're] called to be this, that, or the other thing, when they never really actually thought about it. So, one of the things I really want to have happen is to actually think about what it is that God wants for us. If that creates movement in your vocation, fine. If not, then maybe you can just see your vocation as a way to pay bills and to get your calling done. And that's okay, too. Maybe they walk hand-in-hand. You need to discover that.

Rick: You spoke before in our conversations about faithfulness and obedience. Where does that come from?

Jess: That language came out of the opportunity to do the day care. I think that's really where that came from. I remember the meeting in our house where we had to make a decision whether or not we were going to buy the house. We knew it was a gigantic undertaking and that we would have to do it on faith. It just wasn't going to work otherwise. And so we jumped, we went with it. We did the right thing, but it didn't work. And so then, you have to reflect back and ask what the heck happened. Why did it not work, and how much of it was us, and how much of it was just the situation. I'm not of the theological bent that God sort of took us through it on purpose so that we would learn faithfulness. But I am of the theological bent that as we went through it, we did learn faithfulness, and God's intention for us through that was to learn faithfulness. Sometimes you can't measure things in the same terms of success that you can for other things. And for us, looking back, did we do the right thing? Yes. Were we successful? Yes. Did it work? No. And that's okay. You know, that's not how we measure faithfulness , by asking if something worked. It's a hard lesson. It's not an easy pill to swallow, for sure.

Rick: It's not just because you're small, but because you're close, too.

Jess: Yes. And so you've got to have conversations about how that affects you. And those are really hard conversations, because it's like sitting down with somebody over coffee and telling them how their actions affect you and that our faith and our community is so closely knit and tied, that God set it up that we're dependent on one another and him. It's not an accident that it happens. Those are not very fun conversations to have. It's not about guilt trips just because we need somebody to do something, but it's totally about how I need them there. I need them there [in order] to be who I need to be.

Rick: Like family?

Jess: Yes. And there's not an option in terms of whether you feel like coming. You are part of us. And it's played itself out in a lot of different conversations. We're all really busy and running in a lot of different directions, just because we're all normal people. But that leads to questions about busyness, and leads to questions about work schedules, and whether church schedule supersedes work schedule, even. You know, you've got to pay the bills. Like Laura, for instance, she can't come every third weekend to church because she works every third weekend as a nurse. And so, she gets kind of cut off from the body every third weekend. That affects her—it's hard for her. She's not as connected. So we're having to look and see if there are better ways for her to move her schedule around, but that's nearly impossible. So what does the community have to talk about because of that? There's some real "where the rubber meets the road" kind of conversations.

Rick: So let me play the devil's advocate here. With the situation you're describing, the upside to being part of a bigger church is that when someone's gone, you're still surrounded by other people, and that a big church offers all these different places to meet, more offerings during the week to connect.

Jess: Yeah. And that would be convenient for the person that doesn't feel a sense of urgency to put their faith first and foremost above everything else to make decisions on that. So, it's not a matter of making it convenient for everybody to go and be there, it's a matter of our commitment being such that we make decisions about the rest of our lives around the church rather than making our church decisions around the rest of our lives. Does that make sense at all?

Rick: That sounds pretty profound. Spell that out a little bit.

Jess: I guess what I'm saying is that I'm not necessarily interested in making church all that convenient for people. That takes away the hard choices of doing church in a way that requires ultimate commitment and sacrifice from you and your family. If you've got a vast menu of options from the church, then you can sort of pick and choose the menu that fits best for your life. Well, I'm not sure how much you're realizing the sacrifice of your own Christianity when that's the case. It's not something you plug into your calendar, but you plan and live your life around your church, rather than planning church around your life.

Rick: And knowing you, you're not saying plan your life around the church's calendar in the sense that, okay, you've got to be part of this committee meeting, you've got to be teaching this or that, but more in the sense of planning your life around the lives of other people you are committed to.

Jess: Yeah, that's your "church." It's a tug-of-war between the world that we live in and the busyness that it creates, and slowing down long enough to be intentional with one another. Can that ever happen if we are so busy just doing life unchecked from the church? The church has to have a voice in our busyness. It can't be a secondary thought but a primary thought. So, instead of saying you can't come to church because you have this, this, and this—you're saying no to a lot of other things because you're really committed to the group of people you meet with. That is your body. Again, it's not because we want to bring church attendance up so we can check that off in the yearbook of the Church of God or anything. It's because it really matters when people aren't there, and we feel that. It's hard to have church when people are missing. We don't feel like the whole body is there to participate with us. It's horrible when it happens, but it's a really good thing that we feel this way because it speaks to the level of need to meet and gather, for everyone to be there as a part of what we're doing. It's really important that we all hear the same things and have conversations around those things. I value that so much that when people aren't there, it's a real bummer.

Rick: Somewhere during our talks, you said something to the effect that church isn't a place you go to. Would you mind addressing this idea again?

Jess: It represents a renewed mindset that has to do with seeing ourselves as ever connected to God, his Church, and our mission—that the church isn't here to serve me, but I'm here to serve the church, and the church is here to serve the world. To use a double negative, I'm "never not" part of the body of Christ, the Church. It's very much rooted in Old Testament covenant language, "I'll be your God, you'll be my people." God's not off duty, we're not either. Sundays are great days to be Christians, but so are the rest of the days. Sundays are great days to be part of the community we call church, but so are the rest of the days. In both cases, it's probably more important to emphasize the rest of the days.

Rick: Is there anything you can say about calling in general? In other words, one is called to do what?

Jess: You're not called to convert people, but called to serve people. I think that's the best way I can say it. So, that can happen in so many different ways. It doesn't make you programmatic that way, but it makes it personal. That's when you're really being "missional," if you want to put it in those terms. It's not that you're interested in doing missions, but you are a missional person at that point, where you've really got a sense that God's got you here to serve people, and however you make money is beside the point. The church isn't here for us or to serve us and make us happier, to entertain us. But it's helping us to fulfill our calling, and that we're here for the church and the church is here to serve the world. We're in the cycle somewhere.

Rick: When it comes to doing service-oriented things together as a church, you just respond when you become aware of something?

Jess: Exactly. It's one of the beautiful things about not having a bunch of red tape to get through. And we can respond quickly, which is kind of cool. We talk about it at prayer time and you know, everybody gets that wallet out or writes a check and throws some money in the hopper. It's so much closer to home that way than just giving to the church and then have the church divvy it out over a period of time. Then people submit requests and someone has to make a decision on it. We are the church, so it's a little easier that way in that regard.

Rick: I remember you saying in one of our earlier conversations something along the lines that if you grow and get to a certain size, maybe you will start another church. Is that still a piece of your thinking? Does it matter? Is that what you want to see happen?

Jess: I think I want to see a healthy functioning group of Christians that are fulfilling their calling, and sort of let the chips fall where they may. I know that's really ambiguous, and not a very good answer. But I don't know that we are even close to clicking on all cylinders, so it's hard to imagine breaking up what we've got to start something else at this point. We're kind of relying on everybody that is here to be here. It would be hard.

Rick: Might you see it happening if one couple felt called to go do this somewhere else, instead of just splitting the group in half for the sake of multiplying? This would be like commissioning them to go out.

Jess: Yeah. That would be more realistic. We've made enough decisions to be intentional about being with one another that geographically, if it just can't work and we're so spread out, then maybe the people who come from Vancouver can have their own gathering in that way. We'd have to decide whether or not we want to outgrow our house, and what that means when we get to that capacity. We wouldn't want to have too many more people at our house, but there are other people with bigger houses, so there are other places we could go. I think it would still have an intimate feel. It's not that the house is the ultimate statement or an indictment of the church building or anything like that. I want to see us be healthy and just go crazy in a direction that God wants us to go. I'm sure, if that were the case, we would need to think about that stuff.

Rick: So, do you see Winding Road as a healthy, functioning church body?

Jess: Your best-made groups are those that establish healthy rules for combat and learn how to be real with one another. That's a really healthy path to be on. Now, where we're at on that path I think is a moving target from time to time. But that's the only path toward any sort of a future for our group.

Rick: That's an interesting way to put it.

Jess: You know what I mean? That's ultimately the path that leads us straight to Jesus. I'd love to have more people join the journey with us, but we have to be able to model that correctly for them, or we're just sending mixed messages. I think when we get that down, there might be other people who would want to experience that. If so, are we healthy? I don't know, I guess. I'm not so concerned with the answer to that question as I am with whether we are moving forward on the road. And I think we are!

Rick: When six families show up on a Sunday, I can see where you're starting to feel it in your house when everybody is there with their kids.

Jess: Definitely. We hired a babysitter to watch the kids because they are old enough now that it was chaotic having them in with us. That was a hard thing for us philosophically, because we didn't want to pay anybody to do that, but nobody wants to miss what we've got going on either. So, what ends up happening is that one of us goes [upstairs in the house] and teaches a Bible lesson of some sort. And then there's a high school girl we pay to come watch the kids, and she doesn't have a church that she attends, so we paid her to come to ours. Whoever teaches the Bible lesson comes back down and joins us for our discussion That way the kids are still getting some sort of lesson and they're watched and safe.

Rick: Do the kids join the adults at some point?

Jess: Yes. We start downstairs. The childcare folks don't show up until we are about a half an hour into our Sunday morning, and so we sing together as a group, and kind of just share conversation and life. We were starting to have some major destruction upstairs in our house because we've got four-year-old boys running around wreaking havoc on things, a little bit too unsupervised. The logistics are starting to catch up with us a little bit. Before, we just had babies, and that was easier. When we started this thing, everybody was strapped in a car seat and we could look at 'em, and one would cry every once in a while. But we kind of have to act like a big church now because we've got to figure out what we're going to do with them and have it be meaningful for them. It's not just a time for us to come hangout, but they're actually getting the stories and connecting those to their family and the rest of us. It sure does add a different element of weightiness and responsibility to the whole thing, that's for sure. They are old enough now that it really does matter.

Rick: If you're at a big church, you don't have to worry about it as much; you just send them off to a class of some kind.

Jess: It's not like they're a nuisance, but they are a reality. They are a distraction at times, so you just have to wade through those murky waters and kind of understand why churches make decisions in the way they do to create space for everybody. But at the same time, I don't want to segregate all the different groups of the church. So when they are teenagers, will we have a youth group, or do they just kind of come to understand that this is what we do, and this is how we do it? I don't know; we aren't there yet.

Rick: What kind of people were you reading in the early days that influenced your thinking and ideas about church life?

Jess: Some of the emerging church stuff, like McLaren, although I've really gone away from that stuff now. But I kept coming back to Stanley Hauerwas and things in that vein. I'm still so grateful for his very forward thinking theology. I keep returning to that, almost weekly even still. His book, *Resident Aliens,* is probably one of the best books ever written for the postmodern church.[1] It really took me away from the emerging church stuff, and more toward what I think is the model we're trying to live with now.

Rick: Do you think there is some type of biblical . . . I'll use this word lightly . . . "pattern" for church life that is applicable to any genera-

---

1. Hauerwas and Willimon, *Resident Aliens.*

tion, any culture, something like key characteristics? I want to say "pattern," but not in a strict sense, obviously.

Jess: Sure, sure. I guess I pull from a lot of different resources. But I've got the Wesleyan Quadrilateral in my head screaming at me saying we're kind of standing in a stream of 2,000 years of church history and you can't just very well pick and choose how you're going to do it.[2] And it's not like I'm an expert in anything to begin with. There are a lot of people who have gone before me and made a lot of really important decisions. So, you've got to look and ask, "What are the essentials? What are the key elements of what we are doing?" I would probably go back to what every good church planter would, or home churcher especially: the Acts 2 model and meeting together and praying together. They were meeting together as Christians. God added to their number. They didn't go out and sort of seek that, I don't think. They did some really important things in terms of breaking bread together, praying together, studying together, and sharing the things that they had. You kind of have to ask yourself if it is descriptive of the Acts church, or is it prescriptive of everything from then on? I think it's probably a little bit of both. For that time, that culture, and for those people and their histories, they had to do it that way.

Rick: So, what about today's church?

Jess: We're not them and we're not there, and we're not in those cultures with those same things pushing on [us] in terms of their culture and religious persecution. You can't just uncork that and bring it 2,000 years forward and say, "That's the model, that's the way you have to do it." I don't know if that's really effective. Although, I think you pull some of those essential things out and say that the reason it worked for them was because they were committed to God through loving one another, sharing their stuff, breaking bread together, and being intentional about being in one another's lives. Those kinds of things still make sense for today. I'm game, you know—I'm ready to do that. That makes sense to me. So then I

2. The Wesleyan Quadrilateral is a method of theological reflection based on John Wesley's work that draws on four different sources: Scripture, tradition, reason, and experience. See Albert Outler's introduction in John Wesley and Albert Cook Outler, *John Wesley; [a Representative Collection of His Writings]*, A Library of Protestant Thought (New York: Oxford University Press, 1964).

go through my church experiences and ask, "When did that really happen?" I saw a lot of individual families going to the same place, one day a week, and they were still just as disconnected as they were from their coworkers, their own families, and from people they went to church with. I didn't see that as something I could get on board with nearly as much as going back to that Acts model and saying, "Okay, let's unpack that a little bit. Let's put some flesh to it and see if that's more fulfilling for everybody involved, and if it would help people fulfill their calling and serve the people around them.

Rick: Is this your "biblical foundation," the Acts model?

Jess: That's kind of the impetus, I guess, behind why we're doing what we're doing. Ephesians 4 informs us a lot, too, in terms of some having the purpose of building up the people. So I really feel like in that sense, the church is there to build up the people within its walls so that they'll go out and do something and serve. God's given a gift to each and every one of us so that we could give those things away to the people around us. If that's in the context of the church, then it serves to disciple them, or gives them strength in a way they wouldn't have had on their own. If it's outside the church then it serves them to serve the world around them and to show God's love to their peer community and people they work with and their own families who don't know the love of God. I think you can use your giftedness both inside and outside the church walls. They serve two different functions, certainly. I think those are the two main things, so that would be the biblical foundation for most of what we do. My success as a Christian really is hinging on your success as a Christian, making one another better, as iron sharpens iron.

Rick: You referred to Paul and tent-making, that whole thing. You can ask the same thing, is it descriptive of what he did or prescriptive for us?

Jess: Right. I don't know. It just worked in that context. I'm not there, but it behooves me to ask whether it can work for us, and what the benefits and drawbacks are, because it tears me away from doing church stuff. I don't have time like I used to.

Rick: Would you be open to the idea of support if your own faith community came to you and said that they wanted to free you from working full-time in order to spend your time doing church-related work?

Jess: I really feel like God has opened so many doors along the way to get me educated in other ways to fulfill sort of my tent-making so that I can do it this way. In terms of going back to school and getting another degree and changing vocations entirely, that was a tough step to do that.

Rick: I'm not suggesting you should.

Jess: Sure, but it would take quite a bit to move me off of this post, I think.

Rick: Let's say you had a chance to speak at a gathering where you had traditional pastors and church leaders, along with a group of young church planter types that want to do things a bit different, alternative church planting, whatever you want to call it. And you get to address them in terms of working together and respecting one another. What would you say?

Jess: Anytime you start something by reacting to what you don't like, you're not coming from a very good place. I'm not the first guy to come along and do something different and I won't be the last guy, and in reality, I don't think I'm doing things all that different. I think I'm tweaking things a bit. Going back to your question, the biggest thing that I would want to emphasize is that people in every church are "never not" a church. Like I said earlier, this isn't something you go to, it's not a place. It's a people. As such, it should affect the decisions that you make as a Christian and as a follower of Jesus. I just feel like we've made church a location and a service, not a life. You're apart from the living reality of the body of Christ.

Rick: And if I hear you clearly, one can even do some of that tweaking in a traditional setting and that would make a world of difference.

Jess: And that's why I say we're not doing anything really revolutionary. We're doing something on a smaller scale because it feels like it could flesh itself out a little quicker. I needed that. It's sort of selfish, I guess, but I needed church to be the church. The more I discovered about it, the more I realized [the church] wasn't doing that.

Programmatically, we're not doing anything different. We're doing things differently in terms of our relationships with each other. And that's the biggest thing, it's the only thing, really, that we're doing differently. There's lot's of churches that have bi-vocational pastors. That's not different. Everyone meets on Sunday mornings, we're doing that. Everyone has a men's and women's group, we do that. Everyone's got children's programs. We're doing that. Everyone has some outreach of some sort. But the point is, what you do with the time you have when you're together, and how real you're going to be with one another, and how intentional you're going to be about getting it messy a little bit. That's where I think most churches fall short. They let people off the hook a little too soon. We continue to use the jargon like, "This is my business, this is my relationship with God, me and Jesus, and I'll do what I want to do." It's hard to speak truth into people's lives in that regard, if that's the way they are going to approach their faith. And so it gets really messy and hard to have some of those conversations that have to happen to make people better people and better Christians. My success as a Christian really is hinging on your success as a Christian.

Rick: Is this happening for the people of Winding Road?

Jess: It takes a high level of commitment to one another to do that. We have each other. I can say that for everyone in our church, it would take an awful lot for them to leave us. It's not a channel or a station you change if you don't like it. So much about church has been about what I'm entertained by, or what my preference is. It really boils down to that for a lot of people, and they just hop from church to church. So, we don't do anything exciting at Winding Road, and that's okay. People are still coming because that's not why they're here. That's why I feel like there's a sliver of hope that we can give, that if you really try to be intentional with one another, to the point where the lines between friendships and spirituality and church get really blurry, then I think you're in a pretty good place.

Rick: Describe what it looks like for your group to stay committed to one another even when it gets "messy," to use your words.

Jess: We talk about everything in our church from how we spend our money to what we put in our bodies in terms of food. We're kind of like a fat church just like everyone else is, and that's not what God would have for us. That kind of stuff is really touchy. I mean, you start talking about someone's money or their waistline, and all of a sudden people get like, "You're awfully judgmental." But that's the kind of thing we are not willing to shy away from.

Rick: So, why are you choosing to "do church" by going small? I ask this again because you've said that even larger traditional churches could go a long way in the direction you want to go, if they were to tweak a few things. Yet, when I take your story and overlay it on top of fifty other stories I've heard in the process of writing this book, most are choosing to be small because of the conviction that it's easier and more effective to be intentional about relationships in a smaller context.

Jess: I think it's a more advantageous starting point, for sure. You're talking about trying to make what seem like pretty small shifts, but really it would change the whole dynamic of a church. It would take some really difficult conversations to do that in an existing church. And it would be sort of a bloodbath in some ways, and I wouldn't really want to. So you have to ask yourself, "Do I stick it out?" I don't know, because that's a hard call. I tell people all the time to just stick it out and do church where you are, not to jump churches, and be committed. Yet, I've jumped ship to start something different, and so maybe I'm a hypocrite in that regard. But I had to do something different because I was being paid to do something that I didn't want to be paid to do anymore. So it changes the game a little bit.

Rick: I've heard others say that we need a place for the casual church-goer, a place where they can go to stick their toes in the water, so to speak.

Jess: I just don't think they're even there. They're not even at church, but they're at something; a social gathering, perhaps. In their minds they're fulfilling an obligation. And am I being really judgmental? Probably. It's not as cut and dried as I'm making it out to be. But at the same time, I'd rather encounter those people out being themselves than pretending they're doing something that they're not really doing, and messing it up for the people that are trying to do it right, you know? That's part of it, because when you meet as the body of Christ, it is going be odd to people, it is going to be uncomfortable for people. It isn't going to be entertaining. I think about Jesus and how he had to be terribly uncomfortable to be around sometimes, most of the time. And that's what the body of Christ is about. It's very uncomfortable because it calls you to do something you haven't been ready to do, or else you would've done it. Then all of a sudden, you're left with this dilemma of moving forward or rejecting the gospel, and that's a daily decision. Well, how many churches are asking their people to make that kind of daily commitment and that there's real peace behind that? I don't know.

But not everyone has a real relationship that they can turn to and be confronted on issues that need confronting, and called to a commitment of deeper sacrifice and service to one another and to God. That's not what people are finding in churches right now, and that's as revolutionary as I think it gets. And that's what Jesus called his disciples to be. Let the dead bury their dead. Drop everything. Take up your cross and follow me. That's not entertainment, folks. I think of the woman at the well who said, "Here's a man that told me everything I've ever done." You feel so exposed. And why can't there be a place in this world that really embodies Christ in such a way that you are laid bare and exposed before the people who love you. How freeing that would be, how liberating that would be. That is the good news of the gospel. You're not a slave to your sin anymore because there are people there who care about you unconditionally, and who are there to walk through it with you.

AUTHOR'S REFLECTION

We Church

I'm excited about including Jess's story of Winding Road Church of God in this book as one of the four examples of street crossers partnering with traditional ministries. One reason is because I, too, was born on the front pew of a church, like Jess, and on a Church of God pew no less. We're of the same tribe, and I'm just a wee bit proud of that fact. So if any of my Church of God friends are listening in, I think Jess and Winding Road Church of God would do D. S. Warner proud as well.[3] If you're not

---

3. Daniel Sidney Warner is credited by most historians as founding the Church of God Reformation Movement in 1881.

of our tribe, please allow me this moment to celebrate. But I'm positive you, too, will learn something from their journey.

Sit down with Jess for an hour or two and talk about church life. Your ideas about church will be challenged at every turn. He's not confrontational, not with in-your-face kind of arguments. But you will be challenged. And here's why: what he and Winding Road Church of God have chosen to do is nearly impossible! They don't try to win you over with the typical church planting jargon and ideals, using a pep-rally approach to win your support with grandiose notions of building a bigger and better church. It's actually quite refreshing to get that kind of triviality out of the way.

In spite of our bigger-is-better and instant-everything culture, Winding Road Church of God has laid a foundation using two key "bricks" that most of us forget to use, or quickly bulldoze under in our discussions about starting new churches and formulas for church growth. First of all, they have a *commitment to commitment*. Commitment is a rare commodity these days in our consumer culture, and this sadly holds true in our church culture as well. This is not an indictment or a put-down of any one church. It's simply a hard reality that we are faced with. It would seem that our surrounding culture has more influence upon how we understand and implement church life than we care to admit. In a culture saturated with consumerism, our churches tend to reflect some of the same trends, methods, and values of the me-first, shopping mall world that surrounds us. Unfortunately, instead of being societal influencers and a counter-culture, we are often more the "influence-ee" and resemble the culture in which we live. Of course, some resemblance is unavoidable, and I suppose, acceptable. Yet competent missionaries and street crossers seek to understand what aspects of the surrounding culture are benign when it comes to kingdom values, and seek to know what aspects of a culture are contrary to life in the kingdom.

Commitment is like a four-letter word, or a ten-letter word in this case. We can tolerate hearing it used in lofty sermons that stir our sentiments to be better Christians, but when it actually comes down to practice, when we are actually called upon to be committed to relationships, that's another story. And this is particularly true when speaking of commitment on a level that Jess and company desire to experience. It means commitment to a handful of people through deep and intimate relationships, like a family of faith, a people we will go to the ends of the earth for, even when they disappoint or fail us along the way. But it doesn't stop there. Jesus ratchets up the implications a notch or two above where most of us live. It would seem that to be committed and devoted to one another is the same as being committed and devoted to Christ (Matthew 25:40). This should cause every single one of us to stop in our tracks and look back to see where we're coming from concerning how we view one another.

Along with commitment, Winding Road Church of God values *calling*. They firmly believe that each member of the body of Christ has a calling. I'm in total agreement. In its broadest sense, we are all called—commissioned, commanded, and anointed to serve. To serve is to "minister." Every member of Christ's body is a minister, a servant, a "priest." Though "the priesthood of all believers" is a familiar preaching point to many of us, it often goes ignored as we acquiesce to familiar roles, outsourcing our callings to the professionally called ones. Let's turn the page to a new chapter. No more lip service concerning the priesthood of all believers. It's time for real service. Let's embrace our pastors, support them, and show them how much we appreciate their service, and then beseech them to rally the church body around the living Christ in the discovery and release of all our callings to serve. Let's tell them that we want to fulfill our rightful place in the priesthood of all believers. I suspect most of them will be delighted to do so!

So where do we start? Whom do we serve, you might ask. Start by serving your family in Christ, your brothers and sisters. They're your kin. Love them first, and let them love you. Let them help you fulfill your calling to serve by allowing them to serve you. This requires something that goes far beyond exchanging smiles and pleasantries on a Sunday morning. It requires a commitment of love and devotion as loyal and lasting as that of the most functional family. And that's not an easy commitment to make, let alone keep.

Community, fellowship, family, kinship, camaraderie—what do these words have in common? In order for these words to be "fleshed out," all of them have in common the same starting point. One requirement must be met at the get-go before we can ever think about experiencing the potential life laden within each word. It requires being "simply together."

Sounds fairly easy. Get together and community "just happens." Assemble around a pulpit or a Pepsi, a communion table or a coffee table, and church just happens. We tend to think that relationships are forged and the fellowship of the Spirit gushes forth, all because we come together to "do church." Whether you are a traditional churcher or a house churcher, fellowship just happens when you get together. Right? Not necessarily. In some ways, nothing could be further from the truth.

Being simply together is not really as simple as we might first imagine. Just as Jess and Winding Road Church of God have poignantly said, church life is all about commitment, to each other and Christ—no matter what. And that's not easy. That's difficult.

As much as we like to preach it from our pulpits, teach it in our seminaries, and talk about it in our Bible study groups, there's nothing easy about it, about being together as the church, that is . . . if we pursue church life at its highest level. It doesn't "just happen," not without deep commitment, not without a total buy-in to the idea that we need one other in order to be followers of Jesus, to be his corporate body in the world today. Is that truly our conviction? Do we emphatically believe that the only way to be "successful" Christians is to succeed together? If so, then "Lone Ranger Christianity" is out, because it is contrarian to the ways of the kingdom. Pick-yourself-up-by-your-bootstraps spirituality is incongruent with a devote-your-lives-to-one-another kind of faith that screams commitment, no matter what.

Wherever we find a healthy church, wherever we discover a vital expression of the body of Christ, what we find is a "We" church, not a "Me" church. A "Me" church is all about "What's in it for me?" and "What must I do to become a better Christian?" A "We" church is all about "We're in this together" and "What can we do to help each other succeed?" A "We" church is a group of individuals who are more "group" than "individuals." It means following Jesus, together. This is one of the beauties of simple churches. Most are very intentional about putting *we* over *me*. This is particularly true of Winding Road, but not exclusively so. Any church worth its salt aspires to this ideal of being a "We" church. You might be a member of a traditional church that values *we* over *me*. Continue to hold this value high and live it out in the sight of all who would look your way, because being about *we* is a telltale sign that your church is pursuing the way of Jesus.

But let's take another step in a new direction of *we*, traditional and simple churches alike. Reach across the "aisle" and hold hands. Perhaps you've been in a church meeting during a time of prayer and the pastor asked the congregation to step into the aisles to take the hands of their fellow brothers and sisters as a sign of oneness and unity. It's time to step out just a little further into the aisle. Take the hand of a simple church planter, a deacon, a Sunday school teacher, an elder, a pastor; step a little deeper into mutual understanding, servanthood, respect, blessing, and teamwork. Let's first convince ourselves that being a "We" church goes far beyond our familiar surroundings by getting to know and love those in our extended family of faith. And then, just maybe, stepping across the aisle to hold hands in this way will give us the courage to take the first step across the street and hold hands with those we once considered strangers.

Missional Gung-ho-ism

I'm all for recovering our missional identity as followers of Jesus. One way or another, we're all called to be street crossers. But like many great ideas that come down the church pike, they tend to lose their dynamism. Powerful and timely movements of the Spirit tend to be, almost by default, copied and recopied until they become impotent and overdone replicas of the original. Are we in danger of doing this again by trumpeting the charge to be a missional church? "Let's go save the world! Let's get out there and just do it! If you're not a missional church, then you're not a church at all!"

I certainly agree that being missional is definitely a huge part of what it means to be a healthy church. But I think a word of caution might be in order for some of us. Don't let your missional "gung-ho-ism" come before your commitment to one another. Don't be in such a hurry as to let your enthusiasm to the change the world supersede your love and devotion to those you've chosen to "do church" with. Winding Road Church of God has been wrestling with this tension since its inception. We can learn from their journey.

Let's look at it this way: Being missional is our charge, our task. It's included in our marching orders as Christ followers. We've been commissioned to mission. But in order to fulfill our mission, we must have something that enables, empowers, and motivates us to go on the mission and have the wherewithal to accomplish it; something more than just good theology, sheer determination, and will power. We need divine life powering our missional motor. I recently read about an electric car manufactured by Nissan that can travel 100 miles on a single charge. An anticipated burgeoning network of recharging stations will make this vehicle practical and user friendly. In addition to recharging stations about town, home recharging technology will be available. You simply drive home, plug in your car overnight, and it's ready the next day to run up and down the streets again for another 100 miles, more than enough for local commuting purposes.

What we need as local missionaries is a power source, a recharging station, enabling us to run up and down streets and cross them for the cause of Christ. We've been wired for this very purpose. Our Lord has given us orders—the *charge to* go and serve. He has also given us power—the *charge of* his Spirit to fulfill our missional calling and identity. And he has set in motion a network of recharging stations where we can access his renewable and sustainable energy to drive on. What better place is there than home to find a recharging station, where we find a family of faith totally devoted to our welfare, growth, and fulfillment as followers of Jesus? One thing that is common among simple churches, something that should cause traditional churches to celebrate and support, is their intentional effort to "do relationships" well. Are they always well done? Of course not—nobody's perfect—including the church body. So whether a church is small or large, new or old, traditional or simple, they need to do relationships well. Who of us would disagree with this vital aspect of church life?

Pudding & Praxis

Winding Road Church of God understands the vital necessity of recharging, of edifying one another, first and foremost. They are not preoccupied with numbers or growing a big church, numerically speaking. At first glance, this might seem like an excuse for mediocrity or a copout. This is not being evangelical or missional! But Jess was revealingly honest when I asked him about their future plans to multiply their church planting effort. That would be "ideal," he said, but he went on to say that unless they become a healthy functioning family at home, they have little to offer the world around them.

Before we have the respect and right to tell others that loving community is possible for them, experience it firsthand for while. You've probably heard the old saying, "The proof is in the pudding." This saying is actually a shortened version of an adage that makes a little more sense: "The proof of the pudding is in the eating." This is so true, and on several levels. If by pudding we mean the good news of the gospel, the first thing we must do is "prove it" to ourselves. We need to be convinced that the gospel is real, that it "works," that we can actually live this way, the way of Jesus. Have we tested it for ourselves to such a degree that we have no hesitancy to share it with our neighbors across the street? The answer not only rides on whether or not we have proved to ourselves that the pudding is edible, but that it's also good to eat and good for us. This requires group experimentation and discovery in our familial faith relationships. As Jess likes to say, "Church isn't about convenience." It's about commitment, sacrifice, and laying it all on the line for the sake of your family in Christ. If we are unwilling to explore this and fathom the depths of what it means to be brothers and sisters in Christ, then what do we really have to offer those who reject Christianity? Entertainment? A social club?

Once we have come together to prove and experience the substance of our faith—the pudding, if I can say it that way—it is only then that we have the grace to share a bowl of it with those who are suspicious of what goes on in our kitchens and leery of tasting anything we cook up. So then, how do we prove to others that what we have is not only safe, but so incredibly delicious that it's something to die for? We must give a live demonstration by taking the kitchen across the street!

Preparation for ministry in another culture requires packing our bags with everything we need, including the kitchen sink. It might even require driving a catering van to other parts of town, something like Meals on Wheels. My friend, Bryan, came up with the idea of using a "mobile barbecue" as a means of outreach by the men in his church to surrounding lower income neighborhoods. They modified a trailer by installing a large grill, and pulled it by truck into nearby neighborhoods where they cooked and shared their "pudding" with anyone who walked by. Now that's literally taking the kitchen across the street!

If people are reluctant to come through our church doors to see and taste what we have to offer, then we must go to them. But even if we go to them, there's no guarantee that they will taste and eat—not before seeing what we are all about. Too often we invite people into our own dysfunctional church families, and then wonder why they don't see and respond to the "good news." They first need a live demonstration so they can see the reality of people living in redemptive relationships, the kind we claim to experience on our side of the street as functional families. In so doing, we lay bare the evidence, show proof of the reality of the good news of the gospel, all as a result of living in close proximity with those we want to lovingly reach and serve. Hopefully, they will "taste and see that the Lord is good,"[4] for the proof is in the eating.

Church According to Jesus

Here's an easy question to ask, but it requires an answer that's difficult to put into practice: How did Jesus "do church?" Jesus gathered together a rag-tag team of misfits and lived life with them 24/7. That's how he did church. They were simply together. Following Jesus is as much a corporate experience as it is an individual one, perhaps even more so. Most of us live busy lives, but we should gather together as much as possible. By all means, *gather together* for worship and mutual support. But don't forget to *go together* as well, as a consequence of your worship, to express and share your kinship in Christ with those on the other side of the street. The good news of the gospel is about restoring relationships of all kinds, especially between one another and with God. "We" church, in other words. There is a dynamic and transformational dimension of the Christian experience that is only entered into through intimate relationships with other Christians who love Christ and one another. It's an elusive kind of relationship that is missing in many expressions of human communities around the world, a type that becomes the good news for those who are looking for it. There's no avoiding or going around this relational and corporate piece of the gospel if we are to experience the fullness of it—of him.

It almost goes without saying that there is an individual aspect concerning faith and following Christ. Yet we have overemphasized the individual at the cost of losing sight of the corporate. We quickly bypass the importance of being simply together and what that really means and requires of us. God has invited us, through Christ, to enter into a divine relationship, a relationship that the Father and Son have shared since before the foundation of the world (Ephesians 1:4). I can find no better place to begin a search for the basis for our human community than in the love relationship of the Trinity. In this sense, God is community. And it is into this divine community that we are invited by Christ, and it is this divine community that makes possible any authentic human community among God's people.

---

4. Psalm 34:8 (NIV).

For as much as we like to summon evangelistic fervor to persuade people to enter into a restored relationship with God by making a personal decision to accept Christ, there's another relationship we tend to gloss over. It's a relationship that needs restoration through forgiveness and unconditional love, and that is the relationship between you and me. Jesus said, "But if you do not forgive others, then your Father will not forgive your transgressions (Matthew 6:14–15)." Wow! These are the words of Jesus, not of some anti-grace, earn-your-salvation preacher. It certainly would be much easier to plow his exhortation under and to forget about it. Simply praying a prayer of repentance in order to go to heaven when we die is much easier, and not nearly as messy. But this exhortation from Jesus only serves to underscore the eternal significance of restoring relationships. It emphasizes the level of commitment and unconditional love that is required to live as the family of God. If we truly dare to take these words of Jesus seriously, if we dare choose to walk with our brothers and sisters in forgiveness and unconditional love, it will transform our faith communities and churches, and perhaps even the world.

Then . . . just maybe . . . we'll be prepared to cross the street with the reality of the good news of the gospel.

FOR PERSONAL REFLECTION AND GROUP DISCUSSION

1. Jess talks passionately about the significance of being totally committed to the church. What do you suppose he means by this? How have you understood commitment in the past? Is what he's talking about the same thing?

2. How could such commitment begin to transform the church? Think about your own faith community. What specifically might happen?

3. Are there downsides to being overly committed to the church? If so, what are they?

4. How do you define calling? Do you believe that everyone has a calling? Why or why not? Does the church have a corporate calling? If so, what is it? What about for your faith community? Is that calling more specific?

5. Jess believes we are called to serve, both inside and outside the church. When should authentic service be programmed, if ever? Why?

6. If vocation (job or career) and calling are not necessarily the same thing, what are the implications for you personally? How is your job different from your vocation? How might this distinction change things in your local church?

7. If a level of intimacy and depth in knowing Christ is only apprehended through commitment and loving devotion to a family of faith, how might that change things in your life? Where do you have that kind of committed relationship? How would it impact the life of your church and the neighborhood in which you live?

8. Why do you suppose we typically spend most of our allotted church time sitting as an audience or as spectators? Brainstorm about ways to enhance participation in worship gatherings, whether you belong to a traditional church or a simple one. How can you as an individual, and how can your church community, enhance and deepen relationships with others?

9. If you're a simple church planter or leader, how do you respond to Jess's decision in the early stages of church planting to "submit" to something bigger, to be accountable to those who have more experience in ministry even though their experience is from a traditional framework? If you see a need to break free of tradition in order to start something new and different, what will guide you and who will hold you accountable?

4

Simply Go

OF GENES AND JESUS

KEITH SHIELDS GREW UP in a loving family in a rural area east of Red Deer, Alberta, in a farming community known as "Great Bend." The closest town was Delburne, about 180 kilometers (111 miles) north and slightly east of Calgary. They didn't attend church as a family, though his mother was nominally Episcopalian. His father didn't affiliate with any particular denomination. But from the time he was about eight years old, Keith learned about community and faith through a body of believers that loved and nurtured him in his new faith in Christ. "I had a grandmother who prayed for me. She also asked one of our farming neighbors if they would mind getting my sister and me to church. And so this neighbor family used to pick us up and take us to church as small kids." It was a small, rural church, where the community and the church were still intertwined. Keith eventually came to faith at fifteen years of age. Years later, his parents also came to faith, and are now leaders in the same church where Keith first attended at age eight—Great Bend Christian Church. "You look back and see the power of a praying grandmother, you see the power of a community, of a church that embraced me as a young man. You just see the power of God working through a lot of that circumstance."

Just a few years after Keith gave his life to Christ, he was off to Red Deer College in 1977 to study engineering. But with a growing sense of call to ministry, Keith transferred to Alberta Bible College where he graduated with a bachelor's degree in religious education in 1981. He picked up more than a degree at Bible college, however; it's also where he met Maureen. The two of them "tied the knot" the same year he gradu-

ated. In the first five years of their marriage, Keith found himself serving in several ministry roles—as an assistant pastor and youth pastor in
Nanaimo, British Columbia; two years as a lay-leader and part-time pastor for a church plant in Richmond, British Columbia; and two years of
ministry as the lead pastor of Great Bend Church of Christ in Delburne,
Alberta, the church of his youth.

But during this five-year stretch of initiation into the world of ministry and married life, both Keith and Maureen made discoveries about
themselves—as they were growing and maturing as individuals and as
a couple. For one thing, ministry in the church-world brought with it
some difficult doses of reality, quickly dispelling any naïve notions they
held about the glamour and glory of being in the ministry. They had
envisioned setting off on a course of full-time ministry for the rest of
their lives. But these challenging realities fueled Keith's growing desire to
express his calling in ministry and serve God in a "secular" context. So
for the next four years, Keith enrolled at the University of Calgary, where
he earned a Bachelor of Science in Molecular Biology in 1990. It was
also during this time at the university that Keith and Maureen started a
family, which eventually included three daughters.

Something else was birthed during that time: Keith's thirteen-year
second career as a genetic scientist. While working in the genetics lab
at a local children's hospital, Keith was involved in church leadership
as an elder, and participated in small group ministry and worship for
Bow Valley Christian Church in Calgary—a congregation of about 600
people. On occasion, he took on the role of the worship pastor during
the interim periods between worship pastors.

But Keith's desire to meld sacred and secular continued to stir his
imagination. "After thirteen years in the lab, I began to feel a call to plant
a church and do something different." In 2002, Keith was seeking to
become more knowledgeable in the areas of biomedical ethics and community, so his employer at the children's hospital allowed him to take an
unpaid leave of absence from work to further his knowledge base. This
sense of being called to plant a new kind of church came during this
sabbatical period from the lab, giving Keith an opportunity to take some
courses through Regent College in Vancouver. Some ten years earlier,
when he and Maureen were living in Vancouver, Keith had completed
one year of a two-year program of study at Regent. Now he was back at it,
again, but this time with a test tube full of life experiences and questions
about how to do church in a rapidly changing and secularized world.

The "something different" and the desire to plant a simpler kind of faith community had been marinating in his mind for quite some time, eventually taking on the flavor of concepts related to house churches. His understanding of a simple form of church life came from reading books by Robert Banks, Paul Yonggi Cho, Juan Carlos Ortiz, William A. Beckham, Charles Ringma, Wolfgang Simpson, Randy Frazee, Lesslie Newbigin, and Brian McLaren. Keith had been reading about a simple way of being the church for twenty years. Now his study and research on the subject were in high gear—moving him closer to a different kind of church in the real world and not merely in his imagination.

GIVING BIRTH TO NEW CHURCH LIFE

Keith began developing a proposal for a network of house churches that would include a monthly large group gathering. He synthesized much of what he had learned in formulating a vision of a network of house churches, while maintaining an openness and appreciation for more traditional forms of church life. Keith recalls,

> I had thought and dreamed about being part of a house church expression of the body of Christ. I do not believe that this is the only valid expression of the Church. It is one expression amongst many and I believe that it may be very effective in the culture in which we live.

As he began to share this idea with others, there was a growing sense that he should give this idea a try. Bow Valley Christian Church in Calgary, the faith fellowship they had been a part of for the past fifteen years, had developed a vision for planting churches and were looking for a leader to plant their next church. He shared with them the vision he had for planting a house church network, and they chose to support him and the proposed church-planting project.

Bow Valley Christian Church was established in the 1930s and has relocated several times over the years. It is one of the largest Church of Christ congregations in Canada; they are considered a "flagship" congregation and associated with a movement known as the Restoration Movement.[1] Keith's house church-planting project was the second of Bow Valley's church plants. The first project was planted a few years earlier, a Gen-X type church that catered to a postmodern arts commu-

1. For more information about Bow Valley Christian Church, go to http://www.bvccweb.ca.

nity, called Xalt Community Church.[2] Keith comments, "The interesting thing is neither of the daughter churches looks much like the mother church. Bow Valley Christian Church has this idea that we can plant churches and they don't have to look like the mother." They give permission to people to develop church expressions that work in a particular context. For this reason, they were very supportive of Keith's vision for a network of house churches.

A second reason Bow Valley was so supportive of Keith was because they already knew him. Keith had been part of the Bow Valley church family for a number of years and had developed a level of trust within the church community. So supporting him in this new approach to church planting was viewed as less risky because they knew the kind of person Keith was. Though he and the senior pastor, Rick Scruggs, haven't always held to the same perspectives and views concerning ministry, they have always worked closely together over the years.

With the assistance and support of Bow Valley Christian Church, "Connections Christian Church" was conceived and birthed.[3] It started with four families in one house church. Keith and Maureen were the only ones who came from Bow Valley. Two of the families came from another Christian Church congregation, and the other family from a different denomination entirely. In eighteen months' time, Connections grew to four house churches scattered across the city of Calgary. Once every month they came together for a large group gathering in the chapel of a local Bible college.

Being located in the metropolitan area of Calgary, their new network of simple churches came into contact with variety of cultures. Early on, those who got involved with Connections were Anglo-Saxon, Chinese, Filipino, Indian-Trinidadian, and African-Trinidadian. Empty-nester couples, young adult couples without kids, couples with teenage kids, thirty-something singles, and even a widowed grandmother were drawn to what they were doing. They did reach a few couples with young families, but not many. Keith comments, "I would say that in today's consumer culture, it is harder to attract young families away from the exciting programs of large institutional churches."

2. For more information about Xalt Community Church, go to http://xalt.ca.

3. For more information about Connections Christian Church, go to http://www.connectionscc.ca.

As Connections began to develop and mature, Keith found it difficult at times to keep church planting in front of their mothering congregation. Occasionally, Keith returned to Bow Valley with updates for the
leadership and the congregation. Even though the majority of the Bow
Valley congregants was very supportive of their church-planting effort,
at the same time, it was a challenge for some to wrap their heads around
the idea of "doing church" in a different way. Keith believed that as each
church plant experienced some level of success, it would get easier for
people to see that Bow Valley was doing the right thing in planting new
kinds of churches. "How do we go back and tell the good news, the good
stories that have been happening in these other congregations, because
there is a certain amount of [disconnect], and how do we show them
what's going on and keep it fresh in front of them? We're still not sure
how to do that all the time."

During the first few years in the life of Connections, it was mostly
about planting and "building" the church. As time passed, the need for
more pastoral ministry became evident. So in 2007, they brought Cody
Kemper on staff with Connections to share the role of lead minister with
Keith. Cody slowly took on more and more of the lead minister role,
while Keith focused more and more on coaching him and the elders of
Connections Christian Church. This also allowed Keith to begin to look
more and more toward planting another network in another city. They
raised funds for Cody's salary from outside of their regular budget. Other
Christian churches, church planting ministries, and individuals agreed to
supply the funds needed for the sixteen months both of them were on
staff. Cody eventually assumed the duties of lead pastor entirely and continued to build the house church network in Calgary. In the midst of this
growth and transition, Keith realized even more profoundly that his gifts
and passion were better suited to pioneering something new again.

GO WEST YOUNG MAN . . . GO TO VANCOUVER!

Keith researched several Canadian cities and began to pray and wait upon
God to reveal where they should plant the next network of house churches.
In July of 2008, Cody was given responsibility for leading Connections. In
October, they had an official "passing of the baton" at their monthly large
group gathering.[4] And in November of 2008, Keith and Maureen moved

---

4. In the fall of 2009, Michael Coghlin assumed the role of lead minister for
Connections.

to Vancouver, British Columbia—600 miles west of Calgary across the great Rocky Mountains—where they began life again as pioneers in planting simple churches. By phone, Keith continued to coach Cody weekly and talk with the elders of Connections every month.

Their first few months in Vancouver were spent visiting churches—especially in downtown Vancouver— to see what God was already doing in the city, to learn about the culture, and get to know their neighbors. Their goal was also to meet people in Vancouver who might be interested in joining them as part of their core group—people who would resonate with their approach and join their lead team. In the process, they discovered early on that Vancouver had a West Coast mindset, in many ways different than that of Calgary, and that establishing a core group would be more difficult. "I would say Vancouver is a slightly more secularized version of Portland," Keith observes, using an example of a city very familiar to the author. Keith has learned that only about 8.5% of people who live in Vancouver are connected to any sort of church. Keith thinks it's even less for those who live in downtown Vancouver, perhaps even as low as 2%. He further observes, "It's a very secularized city, much more so than Calgary was. Calgary has a bit of a flavor of 'Bible Belt' to it, as close as you get in Canada. But you know that Canada, compared to the US, is a much more secular country." For example, Vancouver is the only place in North America where one can find "safe injection sites" for those who use illegal drugs to inject themselves in a "safe environment." Keith says the city of Vancouver does demonstrate a heart for the homeless and poor, but through very secularized approaches to social issues. He comments, "Kind of like letting everybody do their own thing, even if it's shooting up drugs."

Keith and Maureen settled on the edge of the downtown area, on the boundary between wealth and poverty. Just east of them is the "rougher part" of east Vancouver, and to the west you're into the heart of the business world and condo living. "We think it's a good place to be," Keith remarks. "We'd like to build communities of faith that would actually encompass both types of people and try to learn from each other."

Vancouver is very multicultural. Keith and Maureen learned this quickly and up close; in their own living complex—a condo—thirty percent of the residents are Chinese. Most of the other seventy percent are of European origin with very diverse backgrounds.

Perhaps providentially, two couples from the US—acquaintances of Keith and Maureen—were considering a move to Vancouver for the same purpose of planting a network of house churches. It so happened that these two couples moved to Vancouver all within several weeks of Keith and Maureen's move. It only made good sense to all involved to pool their efforts and resources and work together in the initial phases of planting. They met together as one house church from February to August, and grew to about 25 people and multiplied into two house churches in late August. As of November 2009, Keith and Maureen's faith community, LifeHouse Christian Church, has a core of nine people.[5] The Vine has a core of around eight.[6]

Small in numbers, you might be thinking. Not so impressive. What's the big deal? The big deal is that these two small faith communities are located smack dab in the middle of the city of Vancouver, right within reach of thousands of people who might otherwise go on with their lives removed from any corporate incarnational presence of Christ in their midst. And because they're there, all of God's people elsewhere in the world, especially those who have sent them, are also present. Furthermore, LifeHouse would not be in Vancouver if not for the love, support, and encouragement of their mother church in Calgary. Their adventures in Vancouver are only just beginning, with many streets yet to be crossed for the sake of Christ and for those on the other side.

Q & A WITH KEITH SHIELDS

The following question and answer session with Keith Shields is intended to give the reader more insight into his philosophy of ministry and to address particular issues related to the topic of planting simple churches in partnership with traditional church. Interviews were conducted between March of 2005 and January of 2010, so chronological references in the following interview fall within this time frame. As of June 2011, Keith continues his leadership role with LifeHouse.

Rick: Now that you've been in Vancouver for about one year, what do things look like?

---

5. For up-to-date information about Keith and Maureen Shields and LifeHouse Christian Church, visit their website at http://www.lifehousecc.ca.

6. Visit The Vine at http://www.thevinevancouver.com.

Keith: So far, we largely look like Christians meeting together to figure out what it means to be the body of Christ in this manner and
reach out to our community. Each group has had a few non-church
[people] visit, but we have not made any great breakthroughs yet.
In our core, we have a [thirty-something] couple who were somewhat disconnected from a church in town. They are intelligent,
educated people, who ask really good questions and push me to
consider why I want to do things a certain way. He is [studying] to
be a prosecuting attorney; she is a programmer for a company that
makes video games. They are friends of a friend. We have another
couple who [recently] moved out from Calgary to join us. I taught
[the husband] in a course at Alberta Bible College, and when he
graduated, they decided to join us. We are paying him a half-time
salary. They are a great couple with two kids who do not have much
experience with organic forms of church, so they will be learning
and teaching along with [the rest of] us. I have connected with
many others in our condo tower and in the neighborhood, and
have had people into our home for meals and parties, but so far,
none of the truly "far from Jesus" have joined us.

Rick: How did this core come about?

Keith: Lots of me beating the bushes and praying in the streets.

Rick: So what does it mean to be missional in your specific ministry
and in Vancouver culture?

Keith: Missional, so far, looks like this: Walking with, talking with,
[and] praying with people on the streets of this neighborhood. We
are only eight blocks from the poorest postal code in Canada. I vol-
unteer with COSA Vancouver (a secular organization which sup-
ports and holds accountable high risk sex-offenders upon release
from prison - there are many in the neighborhood). One of the
other guys in LifeHouse volunteers with a palliative care program
and visits with a man who is dying. I volunteered to be the Block
Watch captain for our tower and a few others nearby. The middle
class people of our neighborhood are sometimes afraid of the
criminal types who live close by. So, we get to know each other and
help keep each other safe. I am volunteering with the Olympics and
have met many of the "VANOC" [Vancouver Olympic Organizing
Committee for the 2010 Olympic and Paralympic Winter Games]

employees. I have prayed with one of them who was going through a tough time. He came from an Eastern Orthodox background, but was a purely secular New Yorker. I have had redeeming conversations with many other employees and volunteers. One of the guys in The Vine volunteers at the Community Policing Centre where they do community clean-ups and family movie nights in the park. We are helping pay for counseling for a man who has addictions.

Rick: Have you developed some local relationships with churches and/or pastors that are significant or even critical to what you are doing now?

Keith: Since coming to Vancouver, I have visited many churches and developed many friendships with pastors in the area. I pray weekly with a Southern Baptist church planter. We encourage each other and provide a safe place to vent. I have established a small network of planters who are focused on planting churches by using simple/organic/house structures. I invited around twenty people representing about fourteen different simple church ministries. Eleven of us were able to attend that gathering. We encourage each other, pray together, and talk about common themes.

Rick: Now that you are settled in Vancouver, what kind of relationship do you have with Connections Christian Church in Calgary?

Keith: I am loosely connected to Connections. I try to keep at arm's-length and allow them to find their own way. I talk to each of the elders approximately once a month. One of the elders is on the management team of LifeHouse.

Rick: Looking back on your original development of a proposal for a network of house churches in Calgary, and with what you are doing now in Vancouver, how do you explain the open-minded, progressive attitude of Bow Valley Christian Church?

Keith: A number of the elders had been involved in other church planting organizations. Their senior pastor went on a sabbatical to pray and seek vision for the church. Their church had plateaued at the 500 to 600 mark for a number of years and they were trying to determine how to get beyond their present level of growth. Rick Scruggs, the senior pastor [and part of BVCC for over 25 years], became convinced that they should embark on a journey of planting churches, with a goal of planting a new church every couple of years.

Rick: How is what you did in Calgary as a network of house churches different than a cell-based church that establishes a network of cell groups?

Keith: We believe the main gathering of the church [happens] in homes. On one hand, it's not about what is church, but about being the church. But if you talk about the gathering of the church, the gathering of the body, this local church, this is happening in homes, and will always happen in homes. What we do once a month to bring everybody together, we really don't call that church, the church gathering. That is kind of an additional celebration we do, an additional opportunity to invite people to come and see another side of us. The church happens in homes, and what we mean by that is that everything that was talked about in the New Testament as the elements of a church gathering happens in that home gathering. We spend some time in the word, the Lord's Supper, every time we meet we have a meal together, and we feel that's an important part of who we are. So all of what might be called sacraments of the church happens in the home, such as baptism. Each house church develops a mission.

Rick: Say more about the Lord's Supper and sharing a meal at your gatherings.

Keith: Initially, we said this meal *is* the Lord's Supper—pray at the beginning of it and just eat the meal together and that was the Lord's Supper. But as time went on, we began to realize we wanted a bit more emphasis on the cup and the loaf. And so what has happened now, usually after the main course and before desert or sometimes after, we have someone give a communion meditation. [It's] a thought about the significance of the bread and cup, and we make sure each person has something in their cup at that time, and pass the bread around one more time, and remember Christ in that way. This is kind of a compromise between a meal and the sacramental aspect.

Rick: At one point you said that each house church has its own style. Explain what you mean by that.

Keith: Each house church develops its own style. But as elders and leaders, we also tell them that we think there are some things that need to be a part of their house church; the word, fellowship around the Lord's Supper, opportunity to praise God together, pray together, and there needs to be a mission. These are the elements that need to be part of a house church. But how you work this out is your own expression in your house church. Elders are there as re-source people to help with this and keep you on track, in this sense, but not to be hierarchical or lording anything over you. They are there to help you be the church in your community and to live that out to be the body of Christ where you are. Without some struc-ture, I think it falls apart. With too much structure, yes, it becomes hierarchical, pyramidal, and can be problematic again.

Rick: Describe the process in your thinking and theology of the church, about spiritual formation and evangelism.

Keith: After years of watching the 20% work like crazy while the 80% warmed the pew and observed the show, I realized there had to be something more. I have seen churches emphasize that they will be a cell group church, and I have participated in these churches. But even after our best attempts, we are lucky if we get 40% of our attendance committed to cell groups. One way to help people with their addiction to the show is to stop the show. Bill Henderson has said, "If there's no audience, you know there ain't no show." The opposite is also true, "If there's no show, you know there ain't no audience." Connections Christian Church [and LifeHouse] does not create a show; we create a number of communities where ev-eryone participates.

Rick: Do you see, or do you agree with the idea, that there is potential in traditional churches working together with house church plant-ers, networks, etc?

Keith: We are living proof of this. The Canadian Sociologist, Reginald Bibby, speaks of a need for the church in Canada to be innova-tive if it is to survive.[7] Bow Valley Christian Church has created the freedom and the support for Connections Christian Church to be innovative in our Calgary context [and LifeHouse Christian Church in Vancouver]. They have planted two daughter churches (us and Xalt Community Church). Neither one of the daughters looks like the mother. Both are innovative ways of being the body of Christ in our postmodern world.

7. Reginald Bibby at http://www.reginaldbibby.com.

Rick: Do you see a difference or a variation in the "house church movement" over the past few decades? If so, what do you see as different?

Keith: I have read about the house church movement in Australia and other places. One thing that always struck me was how easily they could become ingrown and comfortable. They became a sanctuary rather than a missional outpost for the gospel. What seemed to be lacking was accountability and connection to the broader body of Christ. I see more accountability and connection in the house church movement of today.

Rick: What do you hope to see happen in the future by way of planting alternative churches?

Keith: The one thing that has become evident is that we really can be a "priesthood of all believers" and be effective for the kingdom. It is not about my superior abilities as a minister. It is about everyone being involved in kingdom work. I don't strive to be the guy who has one message that will fit 600 or more people. We interact together and each one has a message or a song or a shoulder for someone to cry upon. That was part of our vision and desire from the beginning, but we are more committed than ever to this way of operating.

Rick: What is your understanding of the nature of the church?

Keith: First Peter 2:9–10, "But you are not like that, for you are a chosen people. You are a kingdom of priests, God's holy nation, his very own possession. This is so you can show others the goodness of God, for he called you out of the darkness into his wonderful light. 'Once you were not a people; now you are the people of God. Once you received none of God's mercy; now you have received his mercy.'"

Rick: What are the key characteristics of the church needed in your particular setting and culture?

Keith: Canadians are looking for something other than the typical, hierarchical, expensive, institutional church. They want people who are real. They want to share in the life of Christ and not just be told how to live and when to give their money. They distrust institutions and hierarchies. They want something that is real.

Rick: What is your response to the idea that the house church is *the* New Testament model for church life in any given time or culture?

Keith: I believe that this is one model amongst many, but it is a model that has not been sufficiently explored. I support other models of planting. I long for a church that not only brings people in, but also makes disciples of the entire body of believers.

Rick: Is there a "divine" or "biblical pattern" of the church for every generation and culture to emulate? If so, what does it look like?

Keith: Wolfgang Simson speaks of an archetypal form of the church that resides in heaven and implies that house church is that form. I think that this is closer to Greek Platonism than it is to Christianity. I think that God allows us a wide degree of latitude in the forms of the church. Willow Creek is a form that has been used for the advance of the kingdom. The small Lutheran church on the corner near me is another. House church is one way of being the church. It is one way to have a weekly gathering of the local body.

Rick: Do the terms "emerging church" or "postmodern culture" relate to your present context? If so, how?

Keith: Canada (more than the US) is definitely moving toward a post-modern worldview. We are in a period of transition and no one yet knows where this will lead. Brad J. Kallenberg wrote *Live to Tell: Evangelism for a Postmodern Age*. The picture he paints describes very well what we are finding as we participate in evangelism in our context.

Rick: Now you are church planting in Vancouver. I'm assuming your heart, your thinking, and convictions are still along the general lines of the house church type approach to what you're doing. Are you even more convinced of this because of your past experience?

Keith: Definitely. The past five years that we were planting in Calgary has shown us that this is definitely a viable model that we would like to pursue some more here [in Vancouver]. I've now spent some time with other people out here, other pastors, to see what's go-ing on out here. And there are a variety of different models and there are a few people doing some sort of house church type things out here. None of it has really grown rapidly. But we're still very convinced, especially in an urban environment like this. It's really challenging to rent facilities and build buildings or buy buildings. So we think it's one of the ways to go about being the church here in Vancouver.

Rick: What other things did you learn in Calgary that you brought to your new work in Vancouver?

Keith: I would say that we learned in Calgary that when you are planting, you need to be adaptable. You can't just kind of stick to that original plan no matter what. But you also have to keep the core of the vision. So that's how I think we are coming into this [Vancouver plant]. We recognize that we want the core of the vision to be keeping things simple—simple church—whatever that means, and we believe that that's primarily about meeting in homes, or coffee houses, or whatever will work, but keeping things simple. And that we also very much want to build communities that are on a mission together, so communities that want to find ways to be the hands and feet of Jesus into the community. So that's the core of the vision. But we are willing to adapt in whatever ways we need to adapt to this particular culture, to find ways to be the hands and feet of Jesus here in this place. That would be the main thing we've learned from Calgary.

Rick: What would you say to someone who might be wondering if your simple church is actually reaching the unchurched rather than merely rearranging the saints?

Keith: I believe we are actually doing some of both. We are rearranging the saints for mission. That is, we have created spaces where inactive saints have become missionaries to their culture and are reaching their friends and neighbors with the gospel of the kingdom of God.

Rick: Is adaptability a necessary quality to be effective in your work in Vancouver?

Keith: Adaptability has already been necessary. There are so few Christians in downtown Vancouver that we found we needed to build a core by recruiting from Calgary. It may be that I will need to find other work alongside what I am doing to help pay for all of this. Vancouver is not Calgary. We need to be aware of differences and adapt as we go. This is a continual process. Persistence and patience will be needed. Some of the people we have come to reach have not yet arrived in Vancouver. Part of our target audience are the 10,000 people who will move in next door to us in a new community built as housing for the Olympic athletes. They will not begin to move into this new development until next summer. Another 7,000 people will move into another new development that is just being constructed now. Both of these communities are within 800 meters of our home.

Rick: You said, "Let's keep it simple." What's the value in that?

Keith: That does require a little bit of definition because a lot of people have written these days about simple church and things like that, that I wouldn't necessarily even call "simple church." When we're talking about simple, we're saying keep the structures of the church gatherings to a minimum—minimal reliance upon programs, minimal reliance upon staff, minimal reliance upon buildings—and freeing up people's time so that they're not consumed with church activities so that they can engage their neighborhood—get involved on that community association, or get involved on that condo committee, or whatever it might be. We want our people to coach a soccer team—keeping things simple so that they can engage the world and be salt and light into that world. So that's how we would define "simple."

Rick: I suspected that, but I just wanted to hear you say it.

Keith: As opposed to how Thom Rainer would define it or something like that.[8] Organic is probably a good word, too, but you have to define that as well.

Rick: Do you still agree that it's a doable or valuable partnership? I'm assuming you're still connected to Bow Valley?

Keith: Yep. They're still a key supporter. And despite the fact that we've moved to another province and everything, they are still financially involved, they have a member on our management team who over-

8. See Rainer and Geiger, *Simple Church.* The use of the term "simple church" by Rainer and Geiger refers to simplifying the traditional church model in order to move a congregation through the stages of spiritual growth. It should be understood that their use of the term "simple church" is not a reference to alternative church models such as house churches.

sees, they kind of become a team of surrogate elders until we get our own leadership in place here. I think that's one of the things that has been the difference for why we've been able to create networks of house churches, ones that multiplied and grew and were productive, because we had the support of Bow Valley Church and others along the way. But it's that sense of churches that are willing to embrace a model that looks different than they do. They are willing to plant churches rather than clone churches.

Bow Valley continues to support us with prayers and significant finances. The young man from Calgary who has come out to help is the son of the senior pastor. BVCC wanted him to plant a satellite church in Airdrie (a suburb of Calgary), but he chose to come to Vancouver instead. They are very supportive of his decision and the LifeHouse model.

Rick: You spoke of returning to BVCC on occasion to give updates about Connections. Are you doing that for LifeHouse? Did any BVCC people visit Connections and/or LightHouse to experience these churches up close? That's certainly one way of keeping the mother church informed and in touch with what you are doing.

Keith: Yes, I have been back to share with BVCC regarding LifeHouse. They typically have me back once a year to preach and tell the story again. . . . Over the years, several BVCC members have visited both Connections and LifeHouse. We have just come through a rather busy season of this in Vancouver. . . . The chair of the management team, who is also a friend and elder at BVCC, visited with us to see our context again, his second visit. He brought his wife, and although they did not stay for our Sunday evening gathering, they met some of the people and saw our urban context again. This weekend . . . another BVCC elder and his wife are visiting. They previously visited LifeHouse in May. [In] December, another friend from Calgary, originally from BVCC and now a member of Connections, will visit us. There have been several other visits from BVCC friends in 2009.

Q & A WITH RICK SCRUGGS

Rick Scruggs is the senior pastor at Bow Valley Christian Church in Calgary, Alberta. This question and answer session is intended to give more insight into the motivation and goals of traditional churches and their pastors in supporting simple church planters. The interview was conducted in November of 2009.

R. Shrout: I understand that Bow Valley has a vision for church planting. Where does that vision come from?

R. Scruggs: Approximately ten years ago, our leadership at BVCC was frustrated by our inability to grow our church any larger despite everything we tried. We really believed that God wanted every church to grow, but found ourselves stuck on a plateau of about 600 people. We had also been involved with Christian Schwartz of Natural Church Development and his work on church health and realized that one of things we were not doing, that healthy churches did, was involving ourselves in any kind of church planting. From there the vision grew until we decided to commit ourselves to church planting in a variety of ways.

R. Shrout: How do you explain the willingness and commitment of a traditional church like Bow Valley to support the planting of house church networks?

R. Scruggs: Our first plant was a bit unorthodox. We had a Gen-X group that functioned as a "church within our church" meeting on Sunday nights, and we knew that they were getting a bit antsy, so we invited them to be our first plant, if there were interested. They were, and we were off and running. They weren't a "house church," but they weren't like us either, and that kept us from getting stuck on the idea that any plant we did would have to look just like we did. We also realized that there were lots of different kinds of people and different kinds of community, so why not allow the Holy Spirit to shape our church planting effort. We continued to pray about our next initiative and then Keith, who was one of our elders, began to feel God leading him to launch out in a house church model. We didn't know a lot about that particular model, but we loved and trusted Keith and Maureen, and so we threw our support and prayers behind their efforts without any apprehension. The common denominator between our first two plants was that both lead guys had been a part of our leadership team and we knew and trusted them explicitly.

R. Shrout: What kind of process was there when this idea was first presented to the church leaders at BVCC? I'm assuming it may have taken some time or a period of informing and educating the congregation about the legitimacy of house churches and the need to plant them in the surrounding culture.

R. Scruggs: Both lead guys helped our leadership get our heads around their vision. Warren believed in the need for a church that catered to the Gen-X group, and Keith believed in the viability and value of a house church approach. So along with myself and a couple other elders who were risk-takers, we helped the leadership team get on board. Then we began to talk it up at the congregational level, promoting how it fit with our desire to plant more churches, and we didn't really get a lot of flak from anyone.

R. Shrout: What are the greatest challenges in starting and maintaining this kind of partnership?

R. Scruggs: A couple come to mind. One was trying to give these guys freedom to do their own thing, and yet maintain enough contact that they felt supported and encouraged on the journey. We didn't want to micromanage what they were doing, but we wanted to provide some accountability while we were financially supporting them and we wanted them to feel cared for. A second challenge is just how difficult it is to keep the congregation at large connected and interested in the various church plants. The vision leaks quickly and the connection to the new churches was difficult to keep vibrant. The vision to build a new building is so much easier to keep people involved with.

R. Shrout: If you had the opportunity—and maybe you actually have—to stand before a group of traditional pastors and a group of non-conventional simple church planters all gathered together in the same room, what would you tell them?

R. Scruggs: I think it's important to remember that it's going to take all of us and every kind of effort to reach as many people as possible for the kingdom. So it's not either/or, it's both/and. In which case, we need to be supportive of one another's efforts rather than disdainful. Traditional churches need to be open to partnering with simple churches, or perhaps creating a network of simple churches that are spin-offs of their traditional church. In the same spirit, simple church leaders need to realize that some of their simple churches are going to morph into a more traditional look in the years to come, so it might be helpful to prepare for that.

AUTHOR'S REFLECTION

In Search of the Divine Genome

Keith holds a degree in molecular biology and has over a dozen years of experience working in a genetics laboratory. I don't think it's too much to assume that Keith has an inquisitive nature, an analytical mind, and tends to view life around him in terms of elemental and essential components. Assuming this is true of Keith, it doesn't surprise me that he is interested in discovering the elemental components of church life and structures that provide optimal environments for life to flourish and for the gospel to find expression in emerging cultures. And we don't have to be trained in genetics or be church planters to appreciate these same questions about who we are as the people of God, what we are as a community of faith, and what we need to do in order to provide optimal environments for the gospel to have transformational impact in the lives of people.

Let's consider how following Jesus and planting churches has something in common with molecular biology and genetics. A few years ago, there was much attention given in the news about the mapping of the human genome. A thirteen-year project that began in 1990, with the goal of identifying over twenty thousand genes in human DNA, finally determined the sequences of three billion chemical base pairs that make up human DNA. And I thought organizing the desktop on my iMac was a challenge! Understandably, it was a big deal and a major accomplishment in the world of genetics. I asked Keith to explain in his own words what a genome is, exactly:

> In genetics, we define a "genome" as the complete DNA sequence of a single individual organism. The Human Genome Project, headed by Francis Collins [and initiated by James D. Watson], was a work that determined the complete DNA sequence of hu-

mans in general, by sequencing many individuals and comparing the commonalities and differences at each point along a haploid set of chromosomes. Humans are diploid. We carry two copies of each DNA strand. Thus, a human genome, in its simplest definition, is the complete sequence of one of these strands (haploid) along all of the chromosomes of an individual.

Hmm. So you're probably wondering what in the world this has to do with following Jesus, crossing streets, and planting churches. Don't be distracted or confused by all the technical jargon spoken by genetic scientists. Genomes and DNA are quite applicable, really, to our consideration of planting churches on the other side of the street. Let's carry this "genetic" metaphor a bit further and see where it leads.

A Genetically Congruent Lifestyle

A good friend of mine, who is also my chiropractor, is very committed to discovering the key to living life to its fullest—finding a way to live free of disease and stress so that we can reach our created potential as human beings and experience wellness and wholeness as God intended for us. Dr. Dyson talks about pursuing a lifestyle that is "genetically congruent" with the way we have been designed for healthy function as human beings. He states,

> Every living thing has its own unique genetic requirements for health. Maximum health is reached when there is genetic congruency with lifestyle and environment. Humans are the only species that have fundamentally changed their lifestyle and environment *away from* what is genetically congruent. This has resulted in physical, emotional, social, and spiritual brokenness.[9]

If this is true of each one of us as individual human bodies roaming around on planet Earth, is it so far-fetched to think that unique requirements must to be met in order for the corporate body of Christ to reach and maintain its maximum health and vitality? Furthermore, have we as the church moved away from what is genetically congruent? Have we chosen lifestyles and created environments that impede healthy function in the body of Christ and as the church on mission in the world around us? If so, what then, is a "genetically congruent lifestyle" for the people of God?

9. Jamey Dyson. Email communication with the author (November 8, 2009).

"Ark-types" and the Recurrent Image of God

Before going further in raising the question as to what constitutes a genetically congruent lifestyle for the church, there is another term I want to consider that parallels our use of the term genome. Consider the term *archetype* and its various nuances of meaning. In its broadest sense, an archetype is a classic example of something, first of its kind, an ideal representation, a prototype. An archetype serves as a model or pattern for things that follow of the same type. In Jungian psychology, an archetype is an *inherited* memory represented in the mind by a *universal* symbol and observed in dreams and myths.[10] In art and literature, it's a *recurring* image or symbol. For our consideration, I want to suggest the possible existence of an observable divine archetype that recurs in church life, a divine genome that can be mapped along the chain of events throughout church history. And for our use, instead of referring to it as an "archetype," let's refer to it as an "ark-type," particularly in light of the meaning and purpose behind the word *ark*.

In the Bible, we read about several kinds of arks that are illustrative of our discussion. The most recognized ark in Scripture was the vessel built by Noah to save his family and two of every kind of animal from a life-ending flood (Genesis 6:13–15). Another example of a biblical ark was the Ark of the Covenant—another type of vessel. It essentially was a container—a box or chest—that contained the "testimony" of God (Exodus 25:10–21). Interestingly, one of the meanings for the Latin word *arca* is "the chest" or "the place of the heart." Ultimately, some two millennia ago in "the fullness of time," God's rescuing, testifying, proof-giving, heart-revealing ark came to us through his incarnation in the man from Galilee. Jesus was God's original, the first and last, the prototype, the container of divine life, the "exact representation" of his being.[11]

Now let's pull these pieces together and reflect on them for a moment. An ark—a vessel—a sanctuary that serves as a protection against annihilation. An ark—a container—a chest—the heart of God, where he holds us. We are the treasure chest of God for the world to see and behold—his testimony, his evidence, his proof. Similarly, we share Christ with the world who is our treasure secured (held safe) within our "chests" (our hearts). Therefore, I want to suggest that we—the corporate body of Christ—are God's ark, following in the way of Christ—our Prototype. In

10. Jung and Hull, *The Archetypes and the Collective Unconscious.*

11. Galatians 4:4–5; Hebrews 1:3.

Christ, and absolutely because of him, we are the "ark-type" of God—the recurring image and mission of God incarnated—corporately personified—with Christ as head—within human history, culture, and societies. We are the vessel that serves to bring Christ's continuing redemption and healing to the world, to protect the human race against destruction by inviting people to take their place in the divine community—the kingdom—and live in unity as we were originally intended to live.

Lastly, before moving on to address a genetically congruent lifestyle for Christ followers and the church, here's something more to consider: Would the image of God be extinct from the face of the Earth due to the sin of the first Adam—the antitype of God—if not for the righteousness of the second Adam—the prototype of God? I think the apostle Paul believes this to be the case.[12] Furthermore, are we the new human race that comes from Christ, infused with the genome of heaven, and sent forth as the ark-type of God to rescue the world? I'll leave that for you to think about on a rainy day.

A New Testament Prototype?

If the human genome was mapped by determining the sequences of DNA through comparing the commonalities and differences at each point along a strand of human chromosomes, perhaps we can follow a parallel mapping process and try to determine whether or not there is a "divine genome" within church life. If so, can it be "mapped" by comparing the commonalities and differences of the body of Christ along the lines or "strands" of various cultures and times throughout history? If this kind of mapping is possible, what are the common fundamental strands of divine life stretched alongside every living faith community throughout church history? What is the divine genome, the complete spiritual DNA sequence of the body of Christ? Or put another way, what does the ark-type of God look like? What is the recurrent image of God expressed in a myriad of cultures stretching alongside church history through the people of God who follow after Jesus? This is obviously a huge question, one that could occupy the attention of an entire book. There have been books written in answer to other forms of this question, but I wanted to put this question to those willing to cross streets.

---

12. See Romans 5:12–19; 1 Corinthians 15:45–49.

In more or less the same words, I put this question to the dozens of "ecclesial genetic practitioners," the street crossers and simple church planters I interviewed for this book. I sometimes refer to them as "arkitects." I presented the question along the following line: "If you were to step back in time at any point in church history and within any culture where the church has ever existed, are there unique characteristics and markers you would look for to help you identify the presence of the body of Christ? If so, what are they?" What I discovered among them was a similar set of characteristics—a sequence, we could say—of what fundamentally is the church at its essential core. Though not all of the interviewees agreed at every point, they did share in common several characteristics that would help them identify the body of Christ in any historical or cultural context.

There have been several authors in the last few years who have used the miraculous structure and design of human DNA as a metaphor for the mystery and beauty of the life God has imparted to his people, the body of Christ. For example, Neil Cole writes about the DNA of Christ's body in his ground-breaking book *Organic Church*. In short, Cole suggests that this DNA is the same throughout the body of Christ, and that it can be summarized to three elements that are essential for life to thrive in all local church bodies: *D*ivine truth; *N*urturing relationships; and *A*postolic mission—"DNA."[13] Another fascinating use of the DNA metaphor in church life and how it reproduces is found in Alan Hirsch's book *The Forgotten Ways*. Hirsch writes of a discovery he made in his search to answer the question as to how the early church grew so dramatically in the first two centuries. He discovered something he calls "Apostolic Genius"—six components that comprise an inherent "life force" that directs the people of God. Hirsch refers to this as "mDNA" where the "m" stands for "missional."[14] It sure does sound like a type of DNA to me. It also sounds like the presence and work of the Holy Spirit.

One last author I want to cite concerning this DNA metaphor of the church is Leonard Sweet. In his book *So Beautiful*, Sweet suggests that the life of the church is similar to biological life. Church life is helixical like DNA; that is, it has two different strands surrounding a single axis. In the case of church life, a missional and a relational strand spin around an incarnational axis. "The secret of life is the 3-D dance of two

13. Cole, *Organic Church*, 113.

14. Hirsch, *The Forgotten Ways*.

opposing strands, the objective of the missional and the subjective of the relational, which, when they embrace, conceive the incarnational life and the incarnational church."[15] Sweet refers to this "dance" in its corporate expression as an "MRI church." This sounds complex, but it's wonderful imagery, so let's unpack it for a moment.

In the field of medicine, MRI stands for "magnetic resonance imaging." It's a form of imaging or scanning of the human body that allows physicians to view disease or injury to tissues and organs in a particular way that other forms of imaging cannot detect, such as CAT scans and PET scans.[16] These latter two scans have become household words in our home. My wife, Toni, was diagnosed with breast cancer in 1998, and has been battling recurring breast cancer that has metastasized to other parts of her body since 2007. Presently, she undergoes a variety of scans every three months for the purpose of monitoring the efficacy of chemotherapy on eliminating the cancer that seeks to destroy her body.

Let's suppose we could take a "scan" of the corporate body of Christ at various stages throughout the history of the church, thus developing a type of "baseline" reading for church life—a starting point for health. In this case, we are looking for healthy cells, not cancerous ones. And what if we were to compare these scanned images of the church, or lay them on top of each other like transparencies. What would we see? What would we discover?[17] What's really underneath the "skin" of a healthy church? By skin, I mean the external structures and methods of the church that seem transitory with respect to changing times and cultural influences. But what remains the same, and what are the commonalities of any healthy church body? Just as mapping the human genome required comparing commonalities and differences in DNA sequencing, what are the commonalities and differences in church life throughout its existence? More importantly, what are the commonalities that remain consistent over time and context?

15. Sweet, *So Beautiful.*

16. The acronyms might lead one to suspect that these are scans used by veterinarians! They're not. These represent imaging technology used by physicians to detect diseases in human beings, such as cancer. CAT = computerized axial tomography, and PET = positron emission tomography.

17. Sweet writes, "Like body transparencies laid over one another in anatomy class, first lay down the missional, then lay over it the relational, and what forms in the overlay is the incarnational." Sweet, *So Beautiful,* 49.

What Imaging Reveals

Each in his unique way, Cole, Hirsch, and Sweet identify some of the same markers and characteristics of healthy churches that our simple church planters also noted. What are they? It's so profound that it's actually rather obvious and "simple." First and foremost, whenever and wherever we scan the image of the body of Christ, whenever and wherever we map the DNA sequencing of the church, what we see recurring is the resurrected Christ at the center of a living and healthy faith community. As long as Christ is the "head" and vital center of a church body, then it makes little difference as to what kind of church structure it might have, as to what kind of "skin" encloses its internal organs and genetic make-up.[18] Christ must be the center of any attempt at living life together as his followers. Otherwise, every such attempt is no different than any other religious undertaking. The next marker that is always present when the body of Christ is scanned and mapped is loving relationships within the community of faith, and with those on the other side of the street. There has never been an exception to this phenomenon! The third common marker that we notice when we take a closer look at the scans of healthy faith communities is that they think and act missionally, that is to say, they exist for others and not simply for themselves—and they go to wherever "others" live, work, and play. In other words, they always cross streets! And the fourth always-present characteristic that we find in the scans of healthy faith communities is an understanding that effectiveness in ministry comes from being incarnational. They understand that God's "method" to rescue the world takes a vessel, an earthly body, an ark-type—that is, Christ—and now exists corporately for continuing the ministry and anointed purpose of Jesus in the world today and beyond—even to the other side of the street.

I suspect that you, dear reader, whether a member of a traditional church or an alternative faith community, hold in common with our simple church planters the same desire to have these essential elements of church life expressed in your church. Look under your "skin" and see what you find. You might just discover on the inside what has been buried by years of sincere effort to find an answer on the outside. No structure, no program, no eloquent preacher holds the key to your success as a Christ follower or to church growth for your community of faith. No. The answer

---

18. See 1 Corinthians 12:12–13, 27; Ephesians 1:10, 22–23; 4:15; Colossians 2:10. The Greek word *kephala*, usually translated "head," also means "source."

exists in the recurring image and vital substance of life together in Christ. The inherited code, found in the substance of divine life in his corporate body, is without exception; it's always there, always expressed in every human context when the people of God are allowed to pursue a genetically congruent lifestyle. This divine imprint is revealed when people in the body of Christ are simply allowed to flourish and do what they were "wired" to do, to express their internal and eternal design as lovers of God and lovers of people on both sides of the street. So, if you have any say in the matter in your church—let it happen!

What Comes First? Chickens or Eggs, Form or Function?

Now that I've expounded for several paragraphs about the possibility of a divine genome and ark-type inherent in the body of Christ, and have suggested that inherent characteristics be allowed to flourish and express themselves in all our culturally fashioned faith communities, it's time to give a word of caution. If we can actually agree on a handful of time-surpassing, cultural-transcending components of healthy church life, then why the incessant need for some of us to argue over the best way to go about "doing church" and reaching "lost souls" on the outside of our church walls? Some of us have a good case of ecclesial myopia when it comes to defending our understanding of what the church should look like, to the point of delighting in our disagreements with those on the other side. And I'm not referring to those on the other side of the street. I'm referring to those on the same side of the street. They are those on the "other side" of our church experience.

It's been argued thoroughly in church circles before: Which is the best structure, the best form, or the best pattern for church life today? A common angle from which to approach this question, particularly among some house church adherents, is to ask which form is *the* pattern to be emulated based on what we read about in the New Testament and the early testimony of the church. What is the best "type" or "kind" of church? That is, what is the "ark-type?" I used to be one of those asking that very same question. But more recently, I've come to ask another question, not about how to copy the *model* for church life, but about how to know the *life* needed for any church model.

Some would have you believe that a complete overhaul or dismantling of the institutional church is necessary in order to recover the original design of the church, or more pointedly, to uncover the pattern for

God's church that has been buried by centuries of institutionalization, by choosing a lifestyle for the church that has not been congruent with God's original intentions for followers of Jesus. If this describes you, if it's your conviction that we need an overhaul in order to get back to God's prototypical design for church life, then go do it—so long as it leads to healthy function in the body of Christ, and not division! But don't expect others to dismantle their church lives and die for your convictions. Those who might disagree with your church-view may well love God and be committed to the kingdom as much as you are, perhaps more so. One can never be too sure of another's motives.

A Good Time For a Chill Pill

It might be advisable for all of us at this point to just "back off" and let others follow their convictions. Perhaps you are on one side of the fence and feel called to be part of a traditional church body. If so, give your best to that body of Christ followers. If you are a church leader in that context, then allow the body of Christ to flourish by encouraging them to pursue a genetically congruent lifestyle. If you are centered around the living Christ, if you value relationships over rules, if you value mission to the world over spiritual self-indulgence, if you dare stay together in love despite disagreement and sentiment for all the world to see, then you are truly an ark-type and carry the divine genome of God in Christ. Seek after a genetically congruent lifestyle together and discover the presence and power of the living Christ—be ye traditional or simple!

As stated several times earlier in this book, I'm particularly tired and weary of the squabbles and infighting among the family of God when it comes to "doing church" (among other things). It's time to ask forgiveness of one another and move on. So, when it comes to the question of form and function, let's cut to the chase of the matter and boil it down to the following admonition: So long as healthy functioning *flows* through any number of church forms, then let us cease from our lambasting and let them flourish! But where church forms *impede* healthy function in the body of Christ, then it's the responsibility of their respective leaders to do whatever it takes to remove religious cancers from these bodies of faith, freeing them to embark on a genetically congruent lifestyle that thrives from the pursuit of loving, committed relationships, and from participating in the mission of God.

This is my attempt to put an end to the argument, though sadly I suspect it won't end here. My attempt to move past this disagreement is, for some, an impasse of gigantic proportions that will forever remain with those who want to be "more biblical" on the subject. Still, being well aware of those who want to be right, let's seek to move past this disagreement and move on as co-laborers together for the sake of the kingdom, for the sake of those who need hope and who desire to discover a new, yet originally intended way to live life. This is one reason I'm so impressed by Keith's story of partnership with Bow Valley Christian Church. It's a remarkable example of a committed relationship. There's something that rings very true in this story. It has the ark-type of the kingdom imprinted all over it.

Nothing Like a Mother's Love

Every time I consider Keith's journey and his relationship with Bow Valley Christian Church, I get extremely hopeful and excited about the future. And I need that burst of hope and excitement from time to time, especially when I consider the effectiveness, or the lack thereof, of the church to connect with people who are increasingly disinterested and suspicious of Christianity and organized religion. So, I get hopeful about the thought of fellow followers of Jesus coming together for the purposes of the kingdom despite their differences. I become very excited about the future when I think of Keith's story, for it helps me imagine the unlimited potential of established churches across North America coming alongside simple church planters with understanding and support. It's like watching a mother wrapping her arms around her beloved children.

Who of us can't appreciate a mother's love? There's nothing like it in the human experience. The care of a mother is foundational and transformational to every child who is nurtured and bathed in unconditional love. I'm convinced this is no less true between a supportive mother church and that of her child—a street crosser—or of any kind of church planter for that matter. It's more than a business agreement, or at least it should be. It's more than a strategic plan of ministry. It's a relationship—between fellow followers and lovers of Christ. It's a relationship between co-laborers in the cause of the kingdom. It's a relationship between individuals who earnestly desire to do the will of God, to proclaim the glorious good news of the gospel. Simply put, it's a relationship between diverse communities of faith; each community full of expectations and dreams, as well as insecurities and doubts. Yet even in light of their differences and diversity, they choose to honor and love the other for the sake of something greater than their respective glory and success. They choose to embrace a common cause by standing together in kingdom work.

When this truly happens, when people come together with diverse church experiences, opinions, and views, one is hard pressed to find supporting evidence more compelling and convincing when it comes validating our existence to a doubting world. Nothing could be more "incarnational," more visible. At the very least, it's an attention getter! To see diverse churches working together and making a difference in the world—rather than making the news through scandals and infighting—is the kind of stuff that authentic testimonies are made of. It's what earns our right to be heard among the ranks of those skeptical and cynical of anything deemed Christian.

As mentioned before, you don't necessarily need a church overhaul in order to make a difference in the changing world around you. What we do need is more loving mothers! No matter how traditional your church might be, how small you might be in people and funding, and even if your coffers and pews have receded in recent years, perhaps for decades, you can still play a direct role in giving birth to a new church, right across the street or on the other side of town. You can do this by supporting and loving your local missionary. It boggles my mind when I consider the vast and untapped potential of mother churches waiting in the wings, longing to give birth to new life. Think of it—a virtually unlimited movement of street crossers—and only because of the willingness of thousands of mother churches to conceive and give their love, support, and encouragement to simple church planters across North America and beyond! They make it possible for street crossers to "simply go."

Spiritual Spurring

The writer of the book of Hebrews nailed it with this admonition: "And let us consider how we may spur one another on toward love and good deeds."[19] What better definition is there for our purpose as a family of faith than to "spur" each other on toward greater respect and appreciation for each other, toward greater incarnational acts of love and sacrifice in the

19. Hebrews 10:24 (NIV).

immediate world around us, toward embodying the presence of Christ to each other and to those on the other side of the street? Remember, it takes two to spur—two partners, two communities of faith. It takes a relationship.

FOR PERSONAL REFLECTION AND GROUP DISCUSSION

1. Regardless of the type of church to which you belong, spiritual spurring is an invaluable function within the body. Where is this most needed in your particular faith community? In what specific ways could you "spur one another on toward love and good deeds?" In what ways could you spur on a street crosser in your neighborhood?

2. If you belong to a traditional church that has struggled to reach new people—particularly those on the other side of the street—do you believe it is possible for you to "mother" another church, especially a simple church planter and a network of simple churches? Why or why not? If you believe it's possible, then consider what Bow Valley Christian Church has done. Would your church be willing to conceive and give birth to a church plant that has no resemblance to your mother church? If so, what is the upside to such an approach? If not, what is the downside?

3. With your own community of faith in mind, what is a "genetically congruent lifestyle" that would enable your church to reach its potential? What about in your own life?

4. Do you agree with the idea that there is a divine genome, an ark-type that recurs in church life? If so, what would you say are the essential elements of church life that mark faith communities throughout church history?

5. Think about and discuss what it means to be the people of God and Christ's corporate body in your specific neighborhood, town, or city. What do you look like to those on the outside of your church community? How do you think those on the other side of the street would describe your church and what your church values?

6. Keith believes that to engage and impact the immediate world around us with the reality of Jesus, keeping things simple in

church life might be the answer. Do you agree with this? Why or why not? In what ways can you "keep it simple" in the life and ministry of your church?

7. Keith noted that churches—even simple churches—can become "a sanctuary rather than a missional outpost for the gospel." What do you think he means?

8. Reflect on and discuss the relationship between a faith community being a "sanctuary" and an "outpost." Is one more important than the other? Can there be, or should there be, a balance? Do you agree with the observation that churches have a tendency to become insulated from the surrounding community in which they are embedded? How would you describe this "tension" within your own fellowship of faith?

Epilogue: Simply Do Something

MAYBE YOUR NEXT STORY

IT HAD BEEN NEARLY four weeks since he had last seen them in church. His voice messages had not been returned. This abrupt disappearance and silence by the Dunmores was the motivating factor that propelled his finger nervously toward their doorbell. "Do I dare call on them unannounced?" he thought to himself. "Oh well. Fire one and full speed ahead."

"Pastor Evan! I'm surprised to see you on a Sunday afternoon." Will looked shocked, standing behind the screen door. Evan piped in quickly, "I hope I'm not interrupting anything, and I apologize for dropping in on you like this without checking with you first. It's just that I've been a bit concerned about you guys, especially since you hadn't returned my phone calls."

"Ah . . . please, come on in," Will stammered.

Will and Desiree Dunmore were fairly new to Past Perfect Church and had been very consistent in their attendance for the past six months. This 180-degree reversal was quite puzzling and disconcerting to Pastor Evan Jellikel. Evan was the eleventh pastor in Past Perfect Church's sixty-six year history, a small congregation of about seventy-five people on a "good" Sunday. The congregation consisted primarily of middle-aged couples and retirees. Evan appreciated having a younger couple in the fellowship at Past Perfect, like the Dunmores. He sensed that everyone else did, too.

"We are the ones who should apologize, Pastor Jellikel. It wasn't right for us to simply cut-off like that and disappear. I'm sure you were concerned."

"You're right, Will. I have been concerned about what was up. I've been asking myself what in the world could possibly be wrong? Did I say or do something to offend you? You know, thoughts like that have been running through my head this past week, so I just decided to come over and find out."

"I can sure understand that," Will responded. "Excuse me as I go to the kitchen and see if Desiree can join us. Would you like some coffee?" Will shouted as he bolted out of the living room. The living room had been recently painted as Evan made note of the masking tape still clinging to the inside of the windows. It was a modest house, but homey and comfortable. Will was an electrical engineer and worked for a local high-tech company that moved to the community five years ago. His wife, Desiree, was a third-grade school teacher with the local school district.

"Do you prefer it black, or would like to doctor it up with some cream and sugar? It's not Starbucks, but it comes free in this house," Desiree said with a big smile on her face.

"Black is fine. Thank you."

Sliding into an Amish-looking rocking chair, Will appeared uneasy. Then he spoke up after a moment of silence, as Pastor Evan appeared to give everyone some space to collect their thoughts.

"I suppose I should come right out with it and tell you why we haven't been in church for a while." Evan anxiously nodded in agreement. "It's nothing personal, Evan. It's not like you're a lousy preacher or anything."

"That's a big relief!" Evan said while comically wiping his hand across his forehead.

"How can I put it? It's just that we simply can't keep going to church when we are growing more and more disillusioned with the whole thing. I'm not sure if I believe in church anymore, or at least the way we go about it. It's hard to explain," Will said with a sense of resignation.

"I sure wish you would try," said Evan. "It would really help me a lot to understand, and probably do you some good, too, if you would unload your thoughts and concerns. Please be perfectly honest and frank about how you feel. I'm paid to hear this kind of stuff," Evan said jokingly.

Desiree jumped into the conversation as if she were bursting at the seams to say something. "First of all, Pastor Evan, it's not just your church, or Past Perfect Church, I should say. We've been Christians a long time and have been in our fair share of churches. But they're basically all the same when you come down to it. You go to church on Sunday, sit in the pew as if you were part of an audience, sing a few songs, hear sermon after sermon, which appear to make no difference at all to the people listening to them, and then we file out and go back to our real lives of everyday affairs. It just seems more and more like a big disconnect for me."

"Me, too. And there are so many other things that bug the heck out of me," Will remarked. Evan sat in the leather sofa listening with great interest. "Please go on," Evan said. "Let me have it!" as he chuckled. This seemed to break some of the tension as the Dunmores laughed along with him.

Will began pontificating. "To be perfectly honest, I just don't see how the church is making a difference in the world, in the communities in which we live. Not really. I mean, we seem to live in our own little Christian bubble, expecting the world to take notice and show some kind of interest in who we are and what we are doing, or not doing might be a better way to put it. It's as though we expect those on the outside to show up at our doorstep eager to join our strange and antiquated religious culture. Who are we fooling?

"Nice word, honey. 'Antiquated.' Wow," Desiree said sheepishly.

Will went on without missing a beat. "I've been on leadership teams and committees before in other churches. I know about being 'seeker sensitive' and all that stuff, but that all seems less and less real to me now, not to mention less and less effective, at least in the churches where Desiree and I have attended. It's as though the goal of the church is to come up with sensational entertainment by putting on professional productions. Or hire the most dynamic public speaker and come up with the best worship team, and that will somehow draw the people in and grow the church. I suppose that works for some people to some degree, but it all seems so artificial, so consumeristic. It just doesn't seem important to me anymore."

"Wow! 'Consumeristic.' Another great word, honey! You're on a roll today," as Desiree broke out laughing. Evan joined in with the laughter, and finally Will broke out with a big grin.

"I really appreciate what you're saying, Will. I take no offense in it. As a matter of fact, this isn't the first time I've heard concerns like these voiced from one of my parishioners."

"Oh, really?" Desiree said inquisitively. "We aren't the only ones?"

"Not at all," Evan replied. "In one way or another, in the last few years, I've heard this concern voiced more frequently, be it from a parishioner, or from a book I might be reading on the state of affairs of the church. There seems to be a growing awareness that something's missing in our take on Christianity and a growing dissatisfaction with church these days."

"We can certainly testify to that," Desiree said with conviction. "But we don't want to be critical of the church as it is. We still have good friends in some of our former churches, people who truly love God and want to follow Christ. I think both Will and I have been negative about the church for way too long, and we want to move beyond this. That doesn't get us anywhere. But we don't feel we can go back either, you know, go back to the way things are presently."

Will joined in. "That's right. I can't do it anymore. I'm tired of all the meetings, the committees, and the church politics. I'm fried. I don't see how you can do it, Evan."

"I must admit, I get tired and frustrated with much of it, too," Evan admitted. "If I can be totally honest with you, I've had some of the same thoughts and concerns as you are expressing. Sometimes I feel like I'm trapped with no way out, that I'm the only one who really cares about the church. At the same time, I feel helpless to bring about any kind of real of significant change to the way we live as a community of faith. I hope you realize that much of what you're saying is no surprise to me."

"We had no idea you felt this way," Desiree replied. "Perhaps in some ways it's even more difficult for you, being that you've given your whole life to the cause of the church."

Evan leaned forward looking at the Dunmores intently to ask them a serious question. "So, what are you going to do now? Do you have a plan of action, or will you simply give up on the church as you have come to experience it in its present form?

Will leaned back into his Amish-looking chair to think for a moment. "What are you going to do now," repeating Evan's question for all to hear. He paused a moment longer. "Well, simply do something, I guess," he said, as if thinking out loud.

"For one thing," Will continued, "we want to spend more time with our friends and associates. It seems the time we spend in many of our church meetings could be better spent outside the four walls of the church in the company of those we desire to reach. Besides, many of our non-Christian friends want nothing to do with organized religion, especially Christianity. They wouldn't be caught dead inside a church building, unless it was their funeral!"

Then Desiree spoke up again. "Will and I feel that our time is a precious commodity and that we want to be more available to mix with those who need the Lord, and not be so focused on getting our needs met at the church, so to speak. There's only so much we can do, and we've decided this is the direction to go for now," Desiree explained.

"I commend you for your missionary perspective and your desire to be good stewards of your time. That's wonderful," said Evan, "but where will you find fellowship with other Christians? And how will you start this new journey?"

Desiree responded with a sense of certainty. "For one thing, we're thinking of inviting people into our home for dinner, along with some of our Christian friends. We know of some believers in our neighborhood who are interested in this sort of thing. That would be one source of fellowship. Kind of like a house church thing, but not overly religious or controlling. Just keep things simple and genuine. And we wouldn't give up on our friends at Past Perfect or attending an occasional gathering or prayer meeting now and then. We would love to have their input and prayer support, I mean, if they don't become suspicious. I hope they understand what we're trying to do. Nothing personal, you know? We love them. But we definitely want to connect more closely with our coworkers, you know what I mean? And our neighbors, too—become more involved in their lives, if that's possible, and show them the love of God through the way we live and care for each other. Who knows what might come from it?"

"Sounds a lot like the New Testament church, at least my take on it," replied Evan. "Things were more simplified, decentralized in terms of leadership, it was very relational, and they had a deep sense of purpose and calling. I think they had a profound belief that when they met together and loved on each other, that Christ was present in their fellowship. Don't get me wrong. It wasn't perfect and they had their share of problems, but we could learn tons from their example. I think it would revolutionize the church as we know it today."

Will got excited and asked, "Evan, do you really think there's hope for the church, I mean for the church to rediscover some of that . . . well . . . some of that deep stuff again, and begin to reach out and make a difference in the world?"

"I certainly hope and pray for such change," Evan said soberly. "I have many days when I think such change is virtually impossible. But talking with you today has raised my hope again that God is up to something. I mean, when we talk about the church we're talking about people, and you two are examples of God stirring the church from its slumber and self-centeredness. So, I want you to know, that instead of being disappointed in the fact that you're frustrated and leaving Past Perfect Church, I'm actually excited for you and have reason to celebrate! It's as though you two are going out as missionaries into our neighborhood, something like sending local missionaries across the street."

Then Evan paused for a moment, as if to reflect on what he just said. "Perhaps . . . if our people understood your vision and passion, we could release you to go with the blessing of our church body. It would be like sending out church planters, if you will, of the house church variety." Then he said excitedly, "That wouldn't be much of a stretch for our people to wrap their heads around. I mean the ladies at Past Perfect love to support missionaries overseas, and they've been doing so for years! The only difference is that you'd be crossing the street, instead of the Pacific or Atlantic."

"That would be so incredible," Desiree said excitedly. "To know that you are behind us and support our decision would be so freeing. And for the congregation to do so would be so awesome!"

"My head is exploding with thoughts of possibilities and potential of where this could lead," Evan said enthusiastically. "So many ideas are flooding my mind right now. I mean, our congregation is small, and so is our budget, yet I'm imagining so many things we could do for you." The confidence level in Evan's voice was clearly rising. "I can't wait to bring this idea up before the board of elders." Will and Desiree looked at each other with jaw-dropping expressions, as if to ask, *Is he serious?* "This has so much potential!" Evan blurted out. "Let's get together next week and talk more about how the church could partner with you to make this a reality."

DON'T SETTLE

This story is fictional. But a story very similar to this one could be the next chapter in the life of your church, if you dare to color outside the lines a little bit and consider such possibilities. "So, now what? What do we do next?" you might be thinking. For starters, like Will said in response to Evan's question, "Simply do something." And "doing something" might actually mean doing nothing, at first. By "nothing" I mean "waiting." Wait before God as a church body and seek the specific answer to your question—together.

I want to first humbly address those of you who belong to a traditional church. Maybe you pastor one, or perhaps you are a denominational leader. In all humility, and with all the passion and intensity that I can express through the written word, please hear this: We have countless churches scattered across the country that have served Christ faithfully and have blessed many people. And yet, many of these same churches are now struggling to keep their doors open. This might describe your church, the one you love and the one to which you've given your devotion. You're not alone as a church if your budget has dwindled and your attendance has declined. Hundreds, if not thousands, of congregations besides yours have encountered similar obstacles. Maybe you've looked for answers and have settled on the notion that there has to be a way to get more people through the doors of your church building. Perhaps, but don't settle for just inviting them to come to you. Haven't you tried time and time again to implement programs and new ideas with the hope of growing your church and reaching new people for Christ? Have those programs and new ideas worked? Perhaps in a small way, but overall I suspect they haven't provided what was hoped for. Whether they have or not, perhaps now is the time to send some of you to them. In short, consider the option of sending and supporting street crossers. You have exactly what they need to succeed. They need you; and you need them.

The potential is mindboggling. Every church body can send and support street crossers; and "support" doesn't necessarily mean financially. Even the poorest of congregations can give vital support in a variety of ways, most of which involve loving and supportive relationships between partnering churches—and those are priceless! Actually, there is a cost involved in building a relationship with street crossers and the people they touch—love. Freely give it as it's been given to you. The supply is unending; never forget that it's God's love. It's the one and greatest resource that every church will never deplete, for God promises to keep the cup full, even to overflowing! Explore the deep cistern of divine love located at the heart of every church body, and you will discover more than enough. You'll discover God's heart, and it's beyond measure. So whether you belong to a thriving megachurch or you belong to a small congregation that has existed for decades, you have the divine wherewithal to make simple church planting possible. Love on a church planter. And while you're at it, find ways to become more deeply involved with them so you can lavish your unending supply of love on those they seek to reach and serve!

And here's a very important concept to remember in order to make a partnership like this work: If you are willing to readily accept the probability that most people your street crossers touch will never walk through your church doors to attend a worship service, if you will heartily embrace this likelihood—then the sky's the limit. Your influence will reach far beyond the doors of your church building.

DON'T SEPARATE

And now here's a humble admonition for you, simple church planter: You are not the only show in town! And I certainly realize you are probably thinking this is a totally inappropriate metaphor, one that makes you cringe at the thought of being a "show." Nevertheless, you are but one piece of the multifaceted body of Christ. And your existence is predicated upon those who have come before you, most of whom identified themselves with traditional church structures, as well as those who walk beside you now. So go forward, yes. But only with great appreciation and respect for your "elders," those brothers and sisters who have given their lives for the cause of Christ and for the sake of the world.

Everyone benefits from the care of loving parents. So, as a church planter, don't think you're better off on your own. Don't separate. I know this is the temptation for some simple house church adherents; but not all. It was for me. There was a time when I wanted to divorce my "ecclesial parents." Everything they did seemed antiquated, ineffective, out of touch, irrelevant, unbiblical, and just plain wrong. Nearly everyone can relate to a time in their youth when it seemed everything your parents did was an embarrassment. They couldn't do anything right. We just wanted to be left alone to do our own thing, and it seemed that the day would never come, a day when we would be totally independent and living on our own in the real world.

But no matter how justified you believe you are in "doing church" differently—even if your assessment of the surrounding culture is accurate and your methodology is relevant—it does not give you the right to disgrace or demean your parents. If this describes you, don't cut yourself off from their influence and care just because you can't relate to some of the things they do. We already have enough ecclesial orphans running around trying to save the world. There are more important things to fight for than being right. And even if you could prove you're right, even if you could define, pursue, and attain the "perfect" church, it's not as important as keeping the family together and defending the right of your brothers and sisters in Christ to hold to different perspectives and to "do church" in more traditional ways. In other words, unity and coexistence trump better ideas at the cost of parental abuse. Our best ideas of what the church should be like lose credibility when based on demeaning evaluations and criticism of the traditional church.

Parental abuse is against the law, the law of love and respect. It goes against what Jesus said was the greatest commandment next to loving God: to love your neighbor as yourself. In this case, love your family in the traditional church as much as you love your better ideas, your culturally adaptive and relevant methodology and church structures. I want to include myself here—let's go so far as to love them *more* than we love our good ideas and our different ways of doing church. That might turn a few heads.

THE FIRST STEP IN CROSSING THE STREET

If starting a partnership is stirring your heart and imagination, then a good way to start cultivating some ideas might be to answer the following questions:

1. Who are the "Desirees" and "Wills" in your congregation? There just might be one or two sitting right behind you on a Sunday morning. If so, how can you identify who they are? What steps can you take to "call them out," so to speak, to let them know the church values their calling, and will release them with a blessing into ministry across the street?

2. Are there simple church planters already at work in your town or city? How can you find out who they are, and in what ways can you help them in their ministries?

3. If you are a church planter, ask yourself, "What relationships have I walked away from that I should restore? Who in the traditional church-world has expressed a strong interest in my ministry?"

4. If you belong to a church, simple or traditional, where are the "streets" in your community that are not presently being crossed? Why not? Who among your faith community will go? How can you assist them?

A DIVINE SIGNATURE

I want to leave you with a "signature." It comes from John White, a simple church planting coach I interviewed in the process of writing this book.[1] When John signs off on his emails, his signature reads like this:

Every believer a church planter

Every home a church

Every church building a training center

Can you see the vast potential expressed in this signature? Pay special attention to the third line: "Every church building a training center." This really gets at the impetus for this book. Every church can support, train, and send. It's that simple. And just think of how many potential training centers we have across North America and beyond: more than enough for the world to see the distinctive and transforming signature of Jesus.

What is a signature? A signature is a person's name written in a distinctive way as a form of identification in authorizing various documents. A signature is simply a "sign" that indicates that something is authentic, that something has been identified with the one who did the signing. I want to suggest that we are that "something." The church is the signature of Jesus. Are we not his distinct way of identifying himself to the world? If so, we must ask ourselves if his handwriting upon us is legible to those around us. No matter what kind of church you belong to, do everything in your power to allow your church to flourish in such a way that it might be identified as belonging to Christ.

At the very least, there are two things I hope you take away from reading this book. Love one another on the "inside" that you might love those on the "outside." That's it, really. Not too profound, not overly complicated. Sounds fairly "simple." It all comes down to loving your Lord through loving one another (relationships), and serving your Lord by serving others (mission). If you can accomplish this within the context of a traditional faith community, or within the life of a simple church, then go do it, and do it well. But even more, take it to the next level. Discover ways of doing it well . . . together . . . as partners in the kingdom.

1. John White at http://www.lk10.com.

Bibliography

Cole, Neil. *Organic Church: Growing Faith Where Life Happens.* San Francisco: Jossey-Bass, 2005.

Hauerwas, Stanley, and William H. Willimon. *Resident Aliens: Life in the Christian Colony.* Nashville: Abingdon, 1989.

Hiroshi, Sugihara. "What is Occam's Razor?" University of California, Riverside. No pages. Online: http://math.ucr.edu/home/baez/physics/General/occam.html.

Hirsch, Alan. *The Forgotten Ways: Reactivating the Missional Church.* Grand Rapids: Brazos, 2006.

Hofmann, Hans. "Hans Hofmann Quotes." No pages. Online: http://www.hanshofmann.net/quotes.html

Hunter, George G. *The Celtic Way of Evangelism: How Christianity Can Reach the West . . . Again.* Nashville: Abingdon, 2000.

Jung, C. G., and R. F. C. Hull. *The Archetypes and the Collective Unconscious.* 2nd ed. Princeton: Princeton University Press, 1980.

Kallenberg, Brad J. *Live to Tell: Evangelism in a Postmodern World.* Grand Rapids: Brazos, 2002.

Kluger, Jeffery. *Simplexity: Why Simple Things Become Complex (and How Complex Things Can Be Made Simple).* New York: Hyperion, 2008.

Minatrea, Milfred. *Shaped by God's Heart: The Passion and Practices of Missional Churches.* San Francisco: Jossey-Bass, 2004.

Rainer, Thom S., and Eric Geiger. *Simple Church: Returning to God's Process for Making Disciples.* Nashville: Broadman, 2006.

Sjogren, Steve. *Conspiracy of Kindness.* Ann Arbor, MI: Vine Books, 1993.

Stetzer, Ed. *Planting Missional Churches: Planting a Church That's Biblically Sound and Reaching People in Culture.* Nashville, TN: Broadman & Holman, 2006.

Sweet, Leonard I. *Jesus Drives Me Crazy!: Lose Your Mind, Find Your Soul.* Grand Rapids: Zondervan, 2003.

———. *So Beautiful: Divine Design for Life and the Church.* Colorado Springs, CO: David C. Cook, 2009.

Trueblood, Elton. *The Company of the Committed.* New York: Harper, 1961.

Wesley, John, and Albert Cook Outler. *John Wesley: A Representative Collection of His Writings.* New York: Oxford University Press, 1964.

Yoder, John Howard. *The Politics of Jesus: Vicit Agnus Noster.* Grand Rapids: Eerdmans, 1972.

Connections

For up-to-date contact information regarding the street crossers described in this book, or to contact the author, visit **www.streetcrossers .com.** At this website, you can read additional stories about street crossers and dialogue and connect with others interested in traditional and simple church partnerships.

www.ingramcontent.com/pod-product-compliance
Lightning Source LLC
Chambersburg PA
CBHW060342100426
42812CB00003B/1098